The Green Howards
in the Boer War

Major-General. T. E. Stephenson C.B.
Commanding the 18th Brigade

The Green Howards in the Boer War
A Yorkshire Infantry Regiment
at War in South Africa
1899-1902

M. I. Ferrar

*The Green Howards in the Boer War: a Yorkshire
Infantry Regiment at War in South Africa
1899-1902*
by M. I. Ferrar

Originally published under the title
With the Green Howards in South Africa 1899-1902

Leonaur is an imprint of Oakpast Ltd

Material original to this edition and
presentation of text in this form
copyright © 2010 Oakpast Ltd

ISBN: 978-0-85706-375-5 (hardcover)
ISBN: 978-0-85706-376-2 (softcover)

http://www.leonaur.com

Publisher's Notes

The views expressed in this book are not necessarily
those of the publisher.

Contents

Preface	7
The Colesberg District	9
Paardeberg	16
To Bloemfontein	30
To Pretoria	39
The Advance Eastwards	49
The Crocodile Valley	60
Pretoria, Ladysmith, and the Rand	72
The 2nd Battalion Mounted Infantry	82
The 4th Battalion Mounted Infantry	97
Appendices	123

Preface

From month to month during the late war, I regularly sent home to the Editor of *The Green Howards' Gazette,* a short letter, descriptive of our movements in the field. These I have now endeavoured to arrange in a more readable and extended form, my object being to place on record some account of the part taken by the old 19th in the recent conflict in South Africa. Lieutenant W. G. Tarbet has kindly given me permission to make use of his letters on the work of the 4th Battalion Mounted Infantry, which were also written for our regimental *Gazette.* They appear almost verbatim.

For the account of the services of the 2nd Mounted Infantry, in which we were also represented, my thanks are due to Major M. H. Tomlin and Private S. Fallowell, as well as to all those who have kindly lent me their photographs or otherwise assisted me.

M. L. Ferrar
Major, Alexandra, Princess of Wales's Own Yorkshire Regiment
Richmond, Yorkshire
20th February, 1904

CHAPTER 1

The Colesberg District

On the outbreak of hostilities with the South African Republics, the headquarters of the 1st Battalion The Princess of Wales's Own Yorkshire Regiment were stationed at Bradford, with a detachment at Sheffield, and in the ordinary course of events were under orders for Aldershot, where two companies had arrived early in November. But on the necessity for further reinforcements being sent to the seat of war, the remainder of the battalion was hurriedly despatched to Aldershot, arriving there on the 17th November. The work of mobilisation was at once begun, and within a week all our reservists had joined. On the 23rd we paraded for inspection by Major-General Kelly Kenny, commanding the Aldershot Division, previous to our departure next day from Southampton in the S.S. *Bonne Castle*.

The total strength on embarkation was 20 officers and 938 non-commissioned officers and men, under the command of Lieutenant-Colonel Henry Bowles. Of this number, 450 were reservists, and 117 had previously served in the Tirah campaign on the North-West Frontier of India with the 2nd Battalion.

We had been detailed to form part of the 5th Division, under Lieutenant-General Sir Charles Warren, but, as it will be presently shown, we never joined his command. The regiment had already sent some representatives to the seat of war, for in October thirty-five non-commissioned officers and men had left England under Lieutenant Tomlin to form part of the northern company of Mounted Infantry. Captain Bulfin, who before the war had been military secretary to Sir William Butler, was already at the front on the staff of Major-General Pole-Carew, and Lieutenant Gunthorpe had gone out with the Royal Irish Rifles. Two other Lieutenants, Caffin and Noble, had sailed with the Indian contingent, and were locked up in Ladysmith: the former was very badly wounded by a shell during the siege, when attached to the Devonshire Regiment, and Noble, who was later on promoted into the Manchester Regiment, was mortally wounded near Bethlehem on the 12th November, 1901.

The voyage to the Cape, with the exception of a short stay at Las Palmas, was uneventful. We had a fine passage, and there was nothing to disturb the daily routine of physical drill for both officers and men, which took place every morning. The ship was a small one, and had barely sufficient accommodation for the battalion, and in the saloon we had only six other officers besides ourselves.

On the 2nd December we were overtaken by the *Norham Castle* with General Warren and Staff on board, and on the 10th sighted the *Carisbrook Castle*, four days out from the Cape. Being anxious to get some news, we altered our course considerably for this purpose, but "all safe and well" was all the information we could extract in reply to our signals.

The *Doune Castle* arrived at the Cape on the 15th December, just three weeks after leaving Southampton, and we disembarked the next day. The disasters of Stormberg, Majersfontein and Colenso had just taken place. Those of us who, on leaving England, thought that they would be too late to see any fighting, had their minds quickly set at rest, and we all realised that we were in for the thick of it

Leaving all unnecessary baggage, together with our band instruments and drums at Cape Town, we entrained on the afternoon of the 16th by half-battalions. After rather a hot and dusty journey, we arrived at De Aar junction on the 18th, and pitched our camp close to the station.

The 2nd Battalion Royal Warwickshire Regiment arrived at the Cape very shortly after us, and followed us on to De Aar, so that there were three battalions altogether in camp, as the 1st Battalion Essex had already been at De Aar for some time. Sir Charles Warren had also come up, but left almost immediately for Durban, where the rest of his division was concentrated. We were, consequently, rather disappointed at finding ourselves nobody's child, with every prospect of doing duty on the communications.

Owing to the number of casualties in Natal, all the officers were ordered to wear the same dress as the men, and a rifle, waist-belt and pouches were served out to each at Cape Town, all swords being placed in store. This idea was carried to a ludicrous extent afterwards, buttons being dirtied and badges of rank taken off, or anything bright that the sun might catch. We, however, did not go too far, and none of us ever removed our badges of rank, whilst the buttons soon got dirty enough without troubling much about them.

The useless valise was also placed in store at the base, and when the battalion took the field, each man simply carried, in addition to his arms and equipment, one blanket rolled on his waist-belt, together with his haversack, ammunition, and Wallace-spade. The latter article did not last very long. As to our greatcoats, they were carried by the regimental transport, and more than half of them were lost on the march to Bloemfontein, owing to the wretched condition of the mules, through want of proper rations. This was partly due to the loss of a large convoy of over 200 wagons near Klip *drift*, which, when proceeding in rear of the army with insufficient escort, was captured by the enemy. Afterwards when the winter came on, an extra blanket was issued, and sometimes both were carried by the men, but this was only on rare occasions, as, for instance, when the transport might have to go a very long roundabout way, or some difficult drifts were anticipated. So that with two blankets rolled on his belt, a man carried with his rifle, equipment, emergency ration, full haversack, and 150 rounds of ammunition, a total weight of some 50 lbs., and this in a tropical climate, with bad or no roads, and a scarcity of water, made marching anything but easy work.

At De Aar there was a huge accumulation of stores of all kinds, which we had to look after, and we had also to take our share in picquetting the hills surrounding the camp. Just at this time it was very hot, the thermometer registering no degrees in the tents. The dust, which was of a very percolating kind, swept over and into everything, and with the hot wind, reminded one forcibly of the Khamseen on the banks of the Nile. The nights, however, were pleasant and cool.

The men were exercised every day for several hours up and down the *kopjes* near the camp, and by the end of the month were getting hard, and ready for the work before them.

Whilst at De Aar three officers and 130 men were specially selected, on account of their various qualifications, to form a Mounted Infantry company, which was, from time to time, supplemented with drafts from the battalion. We were here joined by Lieutenant Gunthorpe, who had come almost straight from Stormberg, having been attached to the Royal Irish Rifles, by 2nd-Lieutenant Neave, on appointment from the New Zealand Mounted Rifles, and by Captain Buckle, South Staffordshire Regiment

We were all very pleased and relieved to get a wire on the 3rd January, ordering us to Naaupoort. Any change seemed a welcome one that took us away from the never-ending dust. We left in two trains the same evening, all of us, officers and men, in open coal trucks. On arrival at Naaupoort next morning, we found that we had to leave three companies, B, C and F, there under Major Fearon, whilst the headquarters and three other companies went on to Arundel, and A and H to railhead at Rensberg.

Rensberg was only a farmhouse, and at that time was occupied by General French as his headquarters. The Boer position from here was about six miles distant, and extended for some miles on either side of the railway.

The headquarters and Naaupoort companies arrived at Rensberg on the 8th and 9th January, having been relieved by the Suffolk Regiment A few days later, H and B companies, under Captain Williams and Captain Buckle, proceeded to Maidar's farm, about 12 miles west of the railway; and two more, A and F, were sent to Slingersfontein, a farm some 15 miles north-east of Rensberg, C and G with headquarters remaining at the latter place.

On January the 22nd, the two companies at Maidar's farm moved with a flying column to Colesberg bridge, but the enemy were found to be occupying a strong position, and the column had to return without having achieved its object, *viz.*, that of destroying the bridge.

General French now transferred his headquarters to Slingersfontein farm, taking most of his force with him. Here we had to furnish two picquets, one of them on a high hill on the west of the camp and overlooking a chain of *kopjes* running still further west The picquet occupying this hill, with which were some 30 of the New Zealand Mounted Rifles, were continually being sniped every day by the enemy, who were occupying the lower-lying *kopjes*. On the 13th, perhaps to distract our attention, our half-battalion camp was vigorously shelled by a "Long Tom," which was in position close to the railway, about 8,000 yards distant Though some dozen or so odd shells fell actually within our lines, no one was touched, as the shells only burst on the ground, throwing up clouds of dust, but we thought it advisable to change our camp more under cover of the hill.

Our company on New Zealand Hill, as it was called, had been reduced by one-half on the morning of the 15th January. At about 10 a.m., heavy rifle firing was heard, and a message was presently received from Captain Orr, who was in command, that the Boers were trying

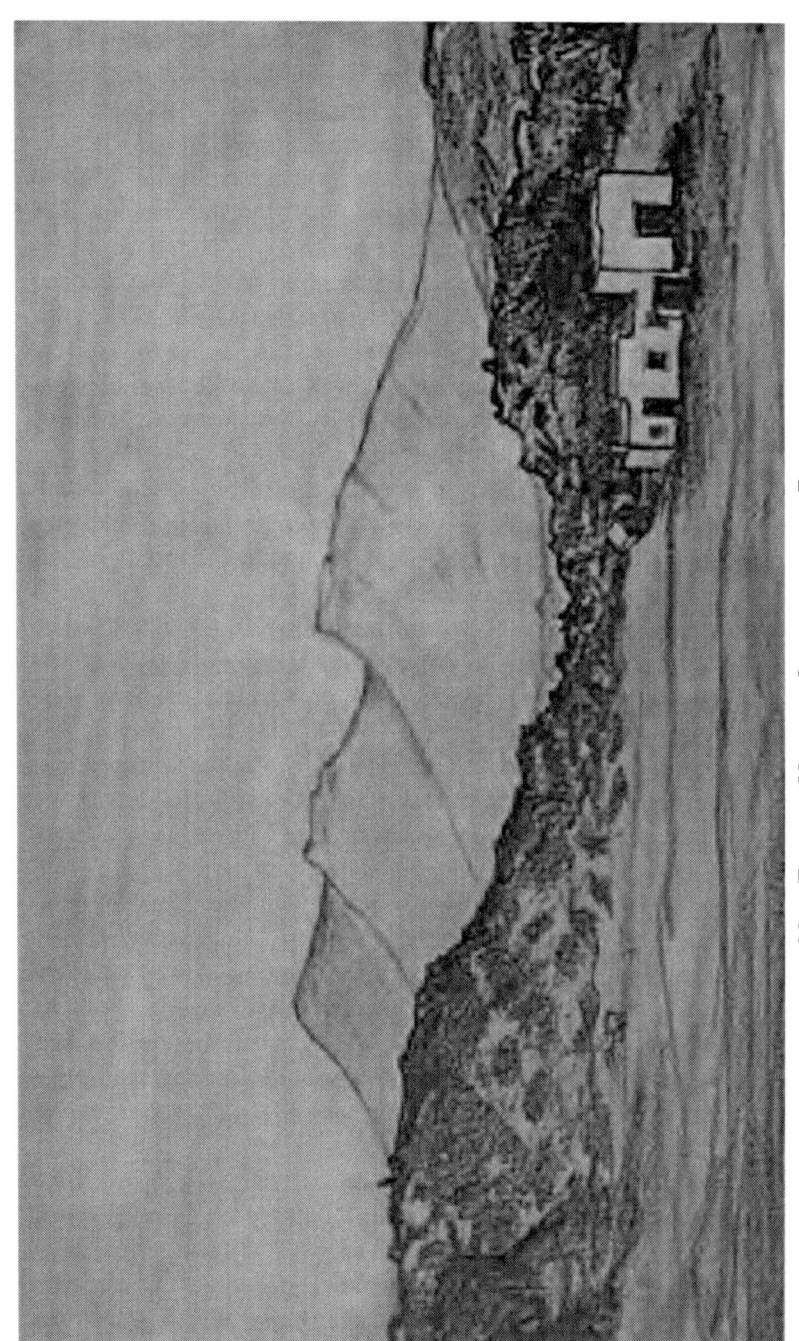

NEW ZEALAND HILL AND SLINGERSFONTEIN FARM

to turn his right flank. On receipt of this message, the remainder of D were sent up, and A and E followed almost at once. The first two were just in time, and a section of A, under Colour-Sergeant Pickard, kept a party of the enemy from working round the left flank, whilst the others did useful work on the top of the hill.

It seems that the enemy had made a most determined attack, and by keeping up a very heavy fire on the *sangars* on the crest line, had tried to rush the dead ground in front of them.

On the firing becoming pretty brisk, some of the New Zealand Rifles who had been in support, under Captain Madocks, R.A., reinforced our detachment, and together drove back the Boers, some of whom had gained the crest, but not before Captain Orr had been severely wounded, whilst Colour-Sergeant Roberts, Sergeant Jamieson, and three men were killed and five wounded.

Lance-Corporal Collings was brought specially to notice for his conduct in heading this charge when all his seniors had been incapacitated. He was afterwards awarded the Distinguished Conduct Medal, but died of enteric later on in the campaign.

We never knew for certain how many Boers were killed in this affair, and we could only find one dead on the top of the hill, but a German whom we met in Pretoria afterwards told us that there were altogether thirty casualties.

The wounded were sent to De Aar hospital, and the dead, seven in all, for two New Zealanders were also killed; were buried in a pretty corner in the garden at Slingersfontein farm, and a wooden cross, with their names, was erected over the grave.

General French ordered D company with the New Zealand Rifles to parade specially, but the company being, unfortunately, again on outpost duty, he asked that his admiration of their gallantry should be conveyed to them. His remarks, he said, applied as well to the New Zealand Rifles. The hill was the key of the position, and of great importance. He had much pleasure in informing both regiments that he had made an official report of their conduct to the commander-in-chief.

Shortly after this, General French transferred most of his force nearer to Colesberg, and on the 22nd January our headquarters, with A and E companies, retraced their steps to Rensberg. Crossing the railway there, they proceeded the next day to Maidar's farm, where they joined B and H. Thence they marched, in company with the 2nd Battalion Wiltshire Regiment, to Hobkirk's farm, distant some 20 miles from Rensberg, in order to take part in some operations the next day. Lieutenant-Colonel Stephenson, of the 1st Essex, was in command of the infantry, and had two companies of his own regiment with him.

We left the farm at 6 a.m., with orders to take and hold a spur on the left-front of the Boer position, in conjunction with the two Essex companies, whilst the Wiltshire Regiment attacked in front.

Our object was to turn the Boers out of their position, which they held north of Colesberg, and to cut their communication with Colesberg road bridge. But there seemed to be great delay in concentrating our force ready for an advance, and the Wiltshires did not come under fire until almost 2.30 p.m. The position, however, was found to be too strong, and though it was turned, our troops were compelled to withdraw in the evening to Hobkirk's farm, as there was no water obtainable nearer.

The Wiltshire Regiment had eleven men wounded, and, although the Green Howards were not under fire this day, it was one of the hardest they had during the campaign, and will not be readily forgotten by any of those who took part in it.

These four companies and our headquarters now returned to Rensberg, and found there awaiting them a draft of 220 non-commissioned officers and men, which had arrived there on the 23rd, under command of Lieutenant Edwards. They filled up the gap in our ranks caused by those who had been taken for service with the mounted infantry.

The other outlying companies had come in, and the whole regiment was once more together, very ragged and weather-beaten, with clothes and boots almost worn out, but cheerful and ready for any kind of work they might be called upon to perform.

CHAPTER 2

Paardeberg

Whilst we were marching and fighting round Colesberg, Lord Roberts and Lord Kitchener had arrived at the Cape, where they were busy perfecting their plan for an advance into the Free State. General French, with his mounted troops, was ordered to the Modder River, and we, together with the Essex and Welsh, followed suit, Major-General Clements, with a weak brigade remaining to hold the Boers in check.

The regiment left Rensberg on the 31st January in a long train of open trucks, the officers being lucky enough to get a covered carriage at Naaupoort. On our arrival there, we found several boxes of pipes, tobacco, and other gifts kindly sent out to us by friends at home. There was also a large consignment of whiskey, which had been forwarded by the Mayor of Bradford as a New Year's present This was much appreciated by the men, and was issued out to them in tots, being a welcome supplement to the ordinary and seldom-issued commissariat rum.

Our experiences in the Colesberg district had shown us how useful it would be if a limited number of field-glasses could be supplied to each company for picquet duty. The Commanding Officer, therefore, wired, asking that some of the money which was being subscribed for the regiment at home might be spent in this way. The result was that each company, for the rest of the campaign, was equipped with four field-glasses, which gave us a greater feeling of security on outpost duty.

We arrived at Modder River station on the 1st February, and encamped on the south side of the River Riet, which joins the Modder at this point We now formed part of the 18th Brigade, which, together with the 13th Brigade, composed the infantry of the 6th Division, under command of Lieutenant-General Kelly-Kenny, C.B. It was made up as follows:

18th Brigade

Brigadier-General T Stephenson, Commanding
2nd Battalion The Royal Warwickshire Regiment
1st Battalion The Princess of Wales's Own (Yorkshire Regt)
1st Battalion The Welsh Regiment
1st Battalion The Essex Regiment

13th Brigade

Major-General C. E. Knox, Commanding
2nd Battalion The Buffs (East Kent Regiment)
1st Battalion The Duke of Wellington's (West Riding Regt)
1st Battalion The Oxfordshire Light Infantry
2nd Battalion The Gloucestershire Regiment

Divisional Troops

Brigade Division Royal Artillery
76th, 81st, and 82nd Field Batteries
38th Company Royal Engineers

The Royal Warwickshire did not join the 18th Brigade till after its arrival in Bloemfontein, it being up to that time one battalion short.

Most of Lord Methuen's force were encamped on the north side of the Modder. He, as well as Cronje, who lay a few miles in front in his trenches, had been practically inactive since the battle of Majersfontein, six weeks before. Had it not been for an occasional shell fired from our advanced lines, and for the balloon which was continually reconnoitring the enemy's position, no one would have thought that the Boers were in our immediate vicinity.

On the 11th February, our brigade got sudden orders to entrain for Graspan, the 13th Brigade at the same time moving by rail to Enslin, another station on the line, and a few miles north of Graspan. We left all our tents standing, and, with the exception of two days at Springfield camp and two at Bloemfontein, we did not live under canvas again till a few weeks after we had arrived in the Crocodile valley, making a period of some ten months bivouacking.

The next day the division commenced its march, with the object of turning Cronje's flank, and in this manner effecting the relief of Kimberley, which had been hard pressed for some months.

The Boer general had at first refused to leave his entrenchments, not realising his position in the slightest, but on becoming aware of our advance, he at last listened to the advice of his officers, and hurriedly quitted his trenches. This turning movement, though it hastened the relief of Kimberley, became, as a matter of fact, a pursuit of the Boer force, for Cronje was *trekking* away in most feverish haste in the direction of Bloemfontein.

Our first march was to Ramdam, on the Free State border, about ten miles distant. Previously to this, all our marching had been performed either as a regiment or by companies. Though we were all as fit as could be, still we felt what a difference it was marching with a large body like a division, with its endless halts and its necessarily laggard pace, all of which only tended to increase our fatigue.

We reached Ramdam at 1 p.m. on the 12th, having started at 6 a.m. that day. There was a good supply of water at this farm, not only from a huge pan, but also from a well near the house, and for the first time since we left De Aar, we came across some of our mounted infantry. Another ten miles the next day, brought us to Waterval *drift*, on the Riet River.

The 18th Brigade crossed the *drift*, which was a very difficult one for the transport, and as we found it impossible to get it over, it was parked on the other side, where we had to send for anything that we wanted.

Our first night march of the campaign now took place. We started from Waterval *drift* at 1 a.m. on the 14th, getting to Wegdrai on the river bank at about noon. Here an afternoon's rest was cut short by the reported presence of some Boers on our left flank, and we had to hurry out in attack formation, only to see no signs of them anywhere. The distance to Wegdrai was 9¼ miles as the crow flies, and it will be evident that marching was very slow, as it took us eleven hours to complete this distance.

We were now asked to make another effort, for it was of great importance to reach the Modder that night. So with the battalion forming the advanced guard, we moved off at 5 p.m. It was dusk at about 7 p.m., and as we advanced we could plainly see the searchlight from Kimberley playing across the sky. We got on fairly well till about 9 p.m., when the stars disappeared, and we felt that a storm was working up. The darkness was intense, and we kept blundering on, tumbling up against ant-heaps and loose rocks, and every now and then someone coming to grief in the many antbear and merecat holes that are so common on the *veldt* Then the storm broke, and to realise a South African storm you must experience it. In about a minute everyone was wet to the skin, and the slippery, muddy *veldt* added further difficulties to the already worn-out foot soldiers, so that Klip *drift*, on the Modder, was not reached until long after midnight A miserably cold night was spent on the river bank, for we had no blankets, as the transport did not arrive till daylight This night march in itself was about twelve miles in a bee-line, but owing to our digressions in the dark, we probably made it much longer. In the twenty-four hours we had already marched ten miles from Waterval to Wegdrai. This, with the addition of the movement against the Boers above referred to, in which two or three miles were covered, was a good performance at the commencement of our divisional experiences.

In the morning the 6th Division took over the defence of the *drift* from General French's troops, who then and there started to relieve Kimberley.

At Klip *drift* a small *laager* had been surprised and captured by the cavalry, and on our arrival many of the tents were standing. Lieutenant Edwards secured for us a most useful shelter, consisting of a long ridge pole and two uprights, which, with the canvas pegged down at the corners and sides, proved invaluable during the rains, and for some time after our arrival at Pretoria we continued to use it as a mess.

We remained at Klip *drift* all day, and nearly all of us enjoyed the luxury of a bathe in the river. On the 16th, the 13th Brigade was ordered out to attack the Boers, who had appeared on our right flank. The fighting lasted all day, and it was then discovered that this rearguard action of the enemy had for its object the withdrawal in safety of the whole of Cronje's force. There were a good many casualties in Major-General Knox's Brigade, amounting in all to about 130 killed and wounded, but the Boer retreat had been retarded, and that was a great matter for us.

We had now to push on, and recrossing the Modder, the regiment bivouacked at Klip *kraal* a few miles further on, as a reinforcement to Colonel Hannay's M.I., who, with some artillery, had taken up a position on some rising ground facing the river.

The division passed by at 8 a.m. the next morning, and we followed, escorting the guns, and arrived at Brandvallei at noon, after a short march of six miles. We halted on the outskirts of what appeared to be a well-to-do farm, which had been deserted by the owners, but not by a considerable number of goats and pigs, chickens and ducks, all of which fell victims to the hungry soldiers. An acre of beautiful grapes, and a large enclosure containing both peaches and apricots, were in a very short space of time, stripped bare of every vestige of fruit, and from a *winkel*, quantities of rice, flour, and groceries were carried away. The men of the 18th Brigade will not readily forget this farm, for it was the first really good one at which they were first arrivals during the campaign. In almost all our other marches, either the cavalry or mounted infantry were always in front, and we had to be content with their leavings. On this occasion, most of the mounted troops were hurrying back from Kimberley.

As every moment now was of the utmost importance, we were only given a brief rest and moved off again, our brigade being still in advance. The ducks were only half-cooked, and the flour only half-baked, and many sighed with regret at having to part with such luxuries.

Lord Kitchener passed the regiment as it moved off, and smilingly spoke words of encouragement to the men. We left Brandvallei just before 5 p.m., and, marching through the night, halted about 1 o'clock on Sunday morning, a few miles from Paardeberg *drift* Here the men simply threw themselves down, pretty well dead beat, to snatch a few hours rest. Up again at 3 a.m., we struggled on, and on reaching the *drift*, were ordered to retrace our steps a short way and to continue our march in an easterly direction. Day had by this time dawned, and very soon we realised that fighting was imminent, as we were ordered to extend our files and to deepen our formation. The regiment was marching as escort to the guns in column of half-battalions, and on reaching the top of the rising ground in our front, we suddenly came upon what looked like a small village on the river bank, about two miles off. The guns at once opened fire on this collection of tents and wagons, for it proved to be the *laager* of Cronje's force; at the same time our two half-battalions swung round somewhat to the left, and deployed into line facing the river. In doing so, we must have shown ourselves very considerably, for we were at once greeted by a heavy fire from the river, distant about 1,500 yards. Our deployment finished, we lay down and awaited orders.

In the meantime, the Essex and Welsh regiments were marching straight to their front, and finally took up a position on the east side of the *laager*. We did not meet again till after the surrender, being attached for orders up to that time to the 13th Brigade.

This reminds us of a similar occurrence in the history of the Green Howards. At the battle of the Alma, when the 19th got separated from its own brigade and joined the left flank of the 1st Brigade Light Division in its assault on the heights, it thereby lost very heavily in killed and wounded. Similarly at Paardeberg, by being detached, the regiment's losses were much heavier than they probably would have been had it accompanied its own brigade. By being detached, it was practically the first battalion of all the force to come under fire from the Boer trenches.

These trenches, with the exception of a few just opposite the *laager* at Vendutie *drift*, were all on the far bank, but this we could not tell at the time, and it was quite impossible at first to discover from which bank the enemy's bullets were coming. It seemed almost a repetition of the Modder River fight, when both banks were held by the enemy, and where there was little or no cover for the assailants.

After we had been lying down under this fire for some time, we were ordered to advance and turn out the occupants of the supposed trenches on the near side.

From where we had halted after deploying, the *veldt* sloped gently down towards the Modder; rough, stony ground it was, with no cover save that of a not-to-be-trusted ant-heap, or an occasional spare boulder or two, and the river bank our objective being 1,500 yards away. The men were beginning to be knocked about pretty considerably, one of the first hit being a man of the machine gun detachment, who evidently offered a good mark to the Mausers concealed amongst the bushes on the edge of the river. Captain Buckle (attached), commanding B company, was one of the next wounded, very badly too, in the neck, and Sergeant Richardson was noticed bandaging him up. But there were soon so many that one could not keep count, and the cry for stretcher-bearers became a frequent one. These, as well as the ammunition carriers, had not an enviable time, but they did their work bravely and well, and Major Ferguson, our medical officer, testified to the skill of the stretcher-bearers' bandaging. Three of them, Corporal Kearns, Bandsman Davis, and Drummer Coombs, were killed, Davis being hit as he was attending to Major Kirkpatrick, who was dangerously wounded in the throat It was quite impossible, therefore, to deal with all the wounded, and the majority of them had to lie out in the sun through all the live-long day before their wounds could be attended to, or before they could be carried to the rear.

Our advance was made by short sectional rushes, the sections working together as far as possible, and directing their fire on the bushes fringing the river, where it was thought the Boers lay hidden in their rifle pits. Their bullets kept falling around us everywhere, but the Boers themselves we never saw all day.

By about 9 a.m. we had advanced to within four hundred yards

SERGEANT A. ATKINSON

of the river. It was about this time that Lieutenant-Colonel Bowles, who was with the front line, was severely wounded in the chest, the command thereupon devolving upon Major Fearon, and soon afterwards an order came that the battalion was not to advance any further. Previously to this, however, a party of about sixty men, headed by five officers, had rushed down to the bank, to find that the Boers were only holding the far bank, and that the river at this point was quite impassable. In this final rush 2nd-Lieutenant Neave and many of the men were killed. Providentially, most of this party happened to jump into some small *nullahs* or *dongas*, and there got comparative cover from the enemy's rifles, which were not more than thirty yards from them. It was here that Sergeant Atkinson went several times for water for an officer and some men who were wounded, and was at last mortally wounded himself in performing these gallant acts. He died a few days afterwards, and his relatives have lately been given the Victoria Cross, which would have been his reward had he lived. Private Burns, who was also with this party, volunteered to go back and stop the firing of a machine gun in their rear, which was making things very uncomfortable for them. He also fully deserved the Victoria Cross, if any man ever did. Sergeant Burgess was indefatigable in attending to the wounded in the *donga*. At night, when all had retired, he voluntarily accompanied the search party down to the river bank on two separate occasions. Many other Green Howards distinguished themselves, and several well-deserved medals were gained by their bravery.

An officer who accompanied this party wrote as follows:

> We had been gradually nearing the river, and when we had got to within about 300 yards of it, we came to a somewhat steeper slope in the ground. Pausing for a space at the top of this to take breath, I called on the men to follow, and we all raced across this intervening ground just as hard as we could go, thinking and hoping that there were some Boers in front of us to get at. I and a lot of the men jumped into a small *donga*, about forty yards from the river. I continued right on, and passed several mimosa trees, till I came to the water, but saw at once that it was quite impossible to cross at this point. Realising this, I thought the next best thing I could do was to have a drink, and I don't think any danger would have stopped me doing this. I had lost my tin mug on the way down, but I lapped up the water with a little saucer I carried in my hav-

ersack, and then handed it to Sergeant Burgess who had followed me. We then returned the way we had come, and had not gone five yards when we found one of the men had been badly hit We dragged him up to the *donga*, but, notwithstanding all our efforts to staunch the blood, he died in about ten minutes. He had been hit in the brachial artery. I now found that Esson and Broun were with me, as well as an officer in the Buffs. Broun had a narrow escape, for as we were attending to the wounded man, a bullet came through the entrance and just skimmed his knee-cap, tearing his trouser. Several more men were hit whilst here. We kept on firing through the bushes across to the opposite bank, where we imagined the Boers to be, for I don't think any of us saw one all day.

By about 2 o'clock I got rather tired of being in this place, and, taking advantage of a slight rainstorm, I ran out with Colour-Sergeant J. Walker and some men, only to find ourselves under a heavy fire, so had to throw ourselves down near a spot where a lot of other men were lying. Here I found Jarvis, and was joined later on by an officer of the Oxfordshire L.I. We remained here till it got dark, when I collected any men I could find and we retraced our steps up the slope, where, finding some more of the regiment, we lay down, all of us utterly exhausted.

Though we hardly saw a sign of a Boer all day, we knew pretty well where they were, and continually directed our fire into the bushes on the far side of the river, where we afterwards found their rifle pits and trenches. The latter were long, narrow, and deep, generally scooped out much wider at the bottom, so that they gave complete cover, unless by chance a shell pitched and burst right inside, which was not likely to happen. Good, sensible trenches they were, on which much labour had been expended, but their dimensions cannot be found anywhere in the manual of Field Fortification.

The roar of the guns and continuous rifle fire was unabated all day. Very early the *laager* was seen to be in flames, and occasional loud explosions told us that some of the enemy's ammunition wagons had blown up.

As those who were closest to the river were unable to cross, and as the remainder of the regiment had been ordered to halt, there was nothing to be done but to remain where we were under a galling fire, a burning sun, and no water for anyone, except for the few who, at the risk of their lives, ventured down to the edge to secure some of the muddy mixture of the river. Several of the men were killed in so doing. All had been without water since the previous afternoon, and what they had started with in their water-bottles had been long since exhausted, probably before the sun went down the previous day.

It was not until dusk that we could with safety collect in groups and make our way back up the slope, where we lay down in different parts of the field, having sent stretcher parties down for any of the dead or wounded that they could manage to pick up, 2nd-Lieutenant Neave's body being among the former. On the roll being called next morning, our total loss was ascertained to be 2nd-Lieutenant Neave, Colour-Sergeant Hughes, Sergeant Tate, and 28 non-commissioned officers and men killed; wounded, Lieutenant-Colonel Bowles (severely), Major T. D. Kirkpatrick (dangerously), Captain Buckle (dangerously), Lieutenant Edwards (severely), and 95 rank and file, ten of whom died of their wounds. Missing, three men. These latter were taken prisoners, and recaptured by us after the occupation of Pretoria.

Such was the part the Green Howards took in the first day's fight at Paardeberg.

The next morning we buried all the dead we could find, and later on, about noon, Lord Roberts rode round our lines to inquire into our losses, being lustily cheered by the men. Shortly afterwards, a message was read to us by Colonel Hickson, of the Buffs, temporarily in command of the 13th Brigade, whose Brigadier, Major-General Knox, had been wounded. It stated that Cronje had surrendered unconditionally, at which we all cheered loudly, but we were much disappointed half-an-hour later to again hear our guns opening on the wretched *laager*. It appeared that Cronje had asked for an armistice to enable the Boers to bury their dead, but this was refused, and unconditional surrender demanded. Cronje's reply was understood to mean that he was prepared to give in, but on being further questioned, he repudiated any intention of surrendering, and the shelling was at once continued.

In the afternoon we were ordered, together with the Gloucestershire Regiment and Oxfordshire Light Infantry, under Lieutenant-Colonel the Hon. A. E. Dalzell, to attack and capture a *kopje* about two miles south of the *laager*, as it was rather a thorn in our side, as well as an obstruction in our surrounding movement. Just before dark, the Gloucestershire men obtained a footing on the eastern side of the *kopjes*, but found the position strongly held by the enemy. The battalions afterwards retained their positions during the night, but were withdrawn at daybreak by order of the field-marshal.

This hill, afterwards so well known to us as Kitchener's Kop, had been at first occupied by Kitchener's Horse, who, on leaving it to water their horses at Osfontein farm close by, found, on their return, that it was in possession of the enemy. It was finally evacuated by the Boers on the morning of the 21st, as their water supply was cut off, and on the regiment being ordered to occupy it then and there, some forty prisoners were captured.

The same day some of us visited the field hospital, about two miles distant on the river bank. The wounded, and there were many, were huddled together in groups under the shade of the mimosa trees that fringed the river. There were a few bell-tents pitched, and in these were the worst cases. Captain Buckle occupied one of them. The bullet had entered his neck, lodging in his shoulder, and his case was considered critical, but, happily, he recovered eventually, although his journey to Modder River station did not help to mend matters much at the time. Major Kirkpatrick had a disagreeable experience, for whilst being operated on, the hospital tent was shelled by a pom-pom, and doctors and patients had to beat a speedy retreat

Kitchener's Kop, which stands about 350 feet above the river, and a little over two miles from it, has a series of under-features running south for about half-a-mile, and on these points, as well as on the higher ones on the north side, we had picquets posted, four companies being detailed for this purpose, the remaining four being in their bivouac in a level space in the centre of the *kopje*. On the morning of the 23rd, at dawn, we were suddenly alarmed by hearing heavy rifle fire close by. On rushing to our arms, we found that our position was being strongly attacked from the south, and we at once reinforced all our posts. Our advanced picquet of a corporal and twelve men had been driven in, and all the picquets were having a very warm time of it. They returned the fire with interest, and with such good effect that in a short space of time a body of about 500 Boers were seen making off across the *veldt*, with our long-range fire to speed them on their way. Those, however, who had driven in our advanced party, still kept up a rapid fire from the strong position they had seized, and also from the bushes at the most southern end of the slope. At about 8 a.m., another body of about 100 were seen to scurry across the open, several of their horses dropping to our bullets, and after this there seemed to be a lull in the proceedings.

Whereupon, Colour-Sergeant Pickard and a party of A company rushed across the open to occupy the small underfeature which the Boers had at first seized, and then evacuated. Immediately on their arrival there, they came under a very hot fire from the scrub below, and two of the men were wounded.

Hearing the firing, some of the Buffs had come up on our right, and B company, supported by F and half of E, were ordered to turn the enemy out of the scrub. In doing so, three officers were wounded, *viz.*: Captain Pearson (severely), Lieutenants Gunthorpe and Wardle (slightly), whilst Sergeant Richardson and eight men were killed, and 17 rank and file wounded.

The Boers, now seeing that all their horses were either killed or useless, decided to surrender, and they gave themselves up to the number of 85. We found eight of their dead on the field, and there were many wounded amongst the prisoners, besides which many wounded no doubt escaped. We also counted 60 dead horses.

The Boers we captured were of all ages, some being old men, others mere boys. We buried our own men together with the eight Boers in one common grave at the south end of the *kopje* the same evening. One of the latter was an old man—any age between 70 and 80 years.

The regiment held Kitchener's Kop up to the 7th March, half the battalion supplying the picquets, the other half the supports, each day in turn. This delay in a forward movement was necessitated by the want of rations and forage, for the capture of the convoy previously referred to, containing ten days' supplies, occasioned a very disappointing halt, and we were, in consequence, on half-rations of biscuits and groceries, and fared only a little better as regards fresh meat We had two biscuits each daily, and about half-a-pound of fresh meat. The latter was bad, and too tough for words or teeth. Goats were given out as rations, four to a company, which, when skinned, were about the same size as hares. There was no tobacco to be had, and matches were very scarce, indeed, half a box fetched as much as 1s. 6d. at the sale of a non-effective kit.

At this period there was a great deal of rain, and it was a common occurrence for the men's bivouacs to be rendered quite untenable during the night, which they had to spend either walking about, or standing waiting for the welcome appearance of the morning sun.

Notwithstanding this, there was little or no sickness amongst them. In one thing we, as a regiment, were very fortunate, for we always had at our command an excellent supply of really good water from Osfontein farm, half-a-mile distant, and were not compelled, like most of the other troops, to drink the filthy Modder water, which, bad as it always is, had been contaminated by the dead bodies, not only of human beings, but also of horses and oxen in every state of decomposition.

It was, very likely, owing to this good supply of water, that we had so few cases of enteric after our arrival at Bloemfontein, as compared with many other less fortunate regiments.

On the 26th, we were warned to be extra vigilant, as it was thought that next day, being the anniversary of Majuba, Cronje would make a desperate effort to break through the meshes that had been drawn around him. However, he does not appear to have had any sentiment of the kind, for on the early dawn of the 27th white flags were flying all over the *laager*, and the good news soon spread that he had surrendered with all his force unconditionally.

Some of us rode across the *veldt* to the *laager* as early as possible, and met the Boers wading across the *drift* and depositing their rifles and bandoliers in a great heap on the bank, before falling in to answer their names a little way further down the stream. It was some time before they all crossed, as they were in no hurry, and took the whole thing very leisurely. There were altogether over 4,000 of them, besides about twenty women and children, whom we noticed near the *drift* Their faces wore a look of supreme indifference to their surroundings, but, surely, it must have been a tremendous relief to get away from their cramped burrows in the river bank, with the incessant noise of the bursting shells, to say nothing of the awful stench of the dead animals! This latter was such that our visit to the *laager* was of very brief duration. Endless confusion of broken and burnt wagons, dead cattle and stores of all kinds, in addition to household effects, scattered about in all directions, describes the scene.

We naturally were on the lookout for some trophies or curios, but beyond the rifles, bandoliers and pom-pom shells, there was little of any interest or value that one could easily have taken away.

There was a semi-circular row of trenches on the north side of the *laager*. These extended for some distance on each side along the bank, but with the exception of the entrance to the *drift*, there were no trenches anywhere on the south side.

After recrossing the *drift*, we rode along the bank past the assembling prisoners, and on to the scene of our advance, which we were naturally anxious to explore. Close by the river we came across seven bodies of our own men, the only way we could distinguish them being by the red patch on their helmets. On our return to camp, a party was at once sent down to bury them.

The Boer wounded, whom we saw in their field hospital a few days later, numbered about 150. Their wounds had not been attended to till after the surrender, and they looked in a very bad way. If we take the ordinary percentage of killed to wounded, their losses were greatly inferior to our own, which amounted to 98 officers and 1,442 men. This, however, is mere conjecture, for many wounded may have escaped after the first day's fighting, and their killed were either all buried or thrown into the Modder.

After the surrender, we remained on Kitchener's Kop on outpost duty, all of us looking anxiously forward to an early advance on Bloemfontein, our great objective, the occupation of which we fondly thought would alter considerably the fortunes of our adversaries, and bring the war to a speedy conclusion.

CHAPTER 3

To Bloemfontein

Whilst the army was quietly waiting for supplies and stores to come up from the base, the Boers were in occupation of some hills, known as the Seven Sisters, about eight miles to the south-east of our position at Kitchener's Kop; every morning our picquets could clearly distinguish the smoke of their camp fires. On the 7th March, Lord Roberts decided to continue his advance on the Free State capital, but preparatory to doing so, the enemy had to be turned out of their position, which was in our direct line of march.

In order to threaten their left flank, the 6th Division left their bivouac at 2.30 a.m., and by dawn had reached Damfontein farm, far enough to show the enemy what we intended, for by this time our mounted troops were working still further round and threatening their rear. They did not wait for this enveloping movement, but continued their retreat eastwards without firing a shot.

As the regiment passed close to one of their *laagers*, we could not help noticing how hurriedly they had cleared off. Their tents, or apologies for such, were all left standing; and coats, rugs, ammunition and entrenching tools were lying about in all directions.

This was a very hard day for all of us. We had been on our legs since 2.30 a.m., and the sun seemed unusually powerful. There was no water to be had; we were all, officers and men, pretty well done up when we reached the Modder at 4.30 p.m. Half-an-hour there for a drink and a rest, and we were on again to Poplar Grove, another three miles along the river, where we bivouacked just as we were, our transport not having come up, nor did it reach us till the next morning. Even in summer, it is astonishing how cold it can be at night in the Free State, and our teeth chattered as we lay huddled together in groups behind the fancied shelter of an ant-heap. It might here be mentioned that during the campaign we, as a rule, carried the men's rations on the transport, and cooked them in bulk by messes in the company camp kettles. It was only on a rare occasion, such as when we thought that the ration wagon might not turn up, that the men were issued with their meat ration uncooked, and this they carried in their canteens, and cooked themselves as best they could. There was a great difficulty in obtaining fuel, and fat for cooking purposes was not to be had. When we were marching on Pretoria, and had halted for the day, the only wood that could be got were the fence posts along the line, and these there was some trouble in securing as there was much competition amongst the different regiments for them, it being a case of "first come, first served."

By cooking the ration in bulk, the men got a better meal and a better cooked one, and there was less waste, with additional comfort

We made a late start next day, not moving off till nearly one o'clock, and reached Wolvefontein just before dark. We heard that both Kruger and Steyn had been here the day before, and had narrowly escaped being captured by the cavalry. President Kruger had come over from Bloemfontein to try and put some backbone into his half-hearted allies, who, we heard, were now wavering all along the line, and were altogether sick of the war. Since then this statement has been repeated more than once, and month after month, as the war progressed, we began to be somewhat sceptical about this so-called "half-heartedness."

We remained at Wolvefontein on the 9th, and resumed our march early next morning, the battalion being told off as right flank guard to the division, which was led by the Welsh and Essex regiments. We were accompanied nearly all the morning by large herds of springbok, which careered about the *veldt* in an aimless manner, evidently terribly alarmed by the numbers of troops all around them. Between the Boers and ourselves on one side, and the Modder River on the other, they were quite hemmed in, and several of them, in an utter state of exhaustion, were knocked over by the men with the butts of their rifles. They would have been welcomed at any other time, but just then there was more serious work on hand.

For the first three hours there were no signs of the enemy, but about 9 a.m. it became known that Abraham's *kraal* was occupied. Remembering the somewhat hurried retirement of the Boers from Poplar Grove on the 7th, few, if any, anticipated anything like a serious engagement The division halted for about an hour, whilst the cavalry reconnoitred the enemy's position. The news soon spread that the Boers were in some force about Abraham's *kraal*, and before long our Horse Artillery came into action against their guns. Our destination was Baberspan, some two to five miles to the south-west of the Abraham's *kraal kopjes*, and General Kelly-Kenny determined to march direct on the former, and so turn the left flank of the latter position, the cavalry sweeping round still further to the south.

This movement exposed our flank and baggage column to attack either from Abraham's *kraal* or the Modder River; Major-General Knox was, therefore, left with a strong rearguard, consisting of the Oxfordshire Light Infantry and the West Riding Regiment, to watch these points, while the remainder of the division pushed forward.

We now found across our road a treble line of *kopjes*, the first little more than undulations of the ground, but gradually rising to a high ridge close to Baberspan, our destination. This formed an ideal Boer position, and quickly divining our intention, he, with his usual mobility, anticipated our slow-moving column of infantry and field artillery in the occupation of these *kopjes*, and established himself strongly across our path. The Welsh Regiment led the advance in the centre, the Essex were on the left, and the Green Howards on the right, the Buffs and Gloucestershire Regiment being in support.

With the assistance of the guns, the Welsh carried the first line of *kopjes* with little opposition. From this point, however, it became evident that we were in for a serious engagement, as from the *kopje* we had occupied on the right we could see that the two battalions on the left had, in their advance, come in for a very heavy cross fire, not alone from the riflemen in their front, but also from the enemy's guns on their flank, and men were seen to be dropping pretty freely. Our brigade was, consequently, ordered to hold the enemy in front whilst an attempt was made to turn their left flank.

In the meantime, however, the day was passing, and as the Boers showed no signs of giving in, the General determined to push forward our brigade, and we got orders to continue our advance at about 4 p.m. We, therefore, left this *kopje*, where we had been under fire for a considerable time, and slightly swung round to our right, moving forward across some open ground, where we came under a very heavy flanking fire, and had some twenty men killed and wounded.

We halted about 800 yards from a long, low-lying *kopje*, which was being shelled by our guns, thus preventing our further advance. Here several more men were hit, and the shelling continued until nearly darkness had set in. We then drew off and bivouacked close by a pan, within easy distance of Driefontein farm, which gave this engagement its name.

The casualties in the Essex and Welsh, who had gallantly charged the main position, were very heavy, numbering in all about 200, whilst ours were comparatively light, being only three men killed and 25 wounded. The total losses in the division were six officers and 52 men killed, and 16 officers and 321 men wounded.

The Boers lost very heavily, 103 dead bodies being found on the field, besides having many wounded. About 20 prisoners were taken, and reliable information since obtained puts their killed at 140 and the wounded at at least 400.

On arrival at our bivouac, search parties were sent out to look for any dead or wounded men, but owing to the large extent of ground over which the battle was fought, the darkness of the night and the rocky nature of the country, many unfortunate men had to wait till daylight before they could be attended to.

On the 11th we marched to Dam Vallei, across an immense dry pan, about two or three miles in diameter, and on the 12th we had another long march, escorting the divisional baggage to Venter's Vlei, the total distance from Driefontein being about twenty-six miles. Nearly all the farms we passed were flying white flags, but, notwithstanding this fact, we approached them with considerable caution. It was during this latter march that we lost most of our greatcoats, as many of the mules broke down on the journey, and, in consequence, the wagons had to be abandoned.

The next day we rested, and did not march off till 3 p.m., and the intention was to make a night march to Brand's Kop, fourteen miles off, which was just a few miles outside Bloemfontein. We made good progress till about 7 p.m., when the sky became overcast, and the moon, which should have appeared by 9 p.m., was not visible, owing to the heavy clouds. Added to this, it commenced to rain heavily, in the middle of which we were ordered to halt on the *veldt* for two solid hours; why, we never knew. Finally, we marched to Brand's Kop in the small hours of the next morning, and bivouacked there in our wet khaki, as uncomfortably as it is possible to imagine.

By this time the men's boots were absolutely worn out and useless, their clothing in rags, and their helmets battered into all sorts of shapes.

In order, therefore, to present as good an appearance as possible on entering Bloemfontein, the most threadbare and disreputable-looking men were placed in the inside fours, so as to escape attention.

At 9 a.m. on the 14th, we started to march into the capital, the 18th Brigade leading, headed by the Essex Regiment, the Green Howards coming next, and the Welsh bringing up the rear. We were one company short, as C company, under Lieutenant Jarvis, had been left behind at Kitchener's Kop on picquet duty, and did not rejoin headquarters till the 17th March. Owing to so many casualties, there were only ten officers who accompanied the battalion on the 14th, *viz.*:

Major J. A. Fearon (Commanding)
Captain M. L. Ferrar
Captain E. M. Esson
Captain B. C. Williams
Captain G. Christian (Adjutant)
Captain C. Organ (Quarter-Master)
Major N. C. Ferguson (Medical Officer)
Lieutenant T. W. Stansfeld
Lieutenant R. H. Darwin
2nd-Lieutenant C. H. Banbury
2nd-Lieutenant E. S. Broun

After marching through the principal streets of the capital, amidst the cheers of the British portion of the spectators, we bivouacked with the remainder of the division about a mile out on the west of the town, at the foot of a low ridge, on which we had to place our outposts.

Bloemfontein is a pretty and peaceful little town. It was regularly laid out, with a market square in the centre, like so many of the other South African towns. It owes its name, not to the flowers that "bloom in the spring," but to a Boer *voortrekker*, named Bloem, and to a spring that he found there.

We had not to wait many days before we were all supplied with new boots and clothing, of which we were in such need. Fresh bread was also served out to us, a welcome change after biscuits. No one who has not been through a long course of these hard, teeth-destroying ration biscuits, can possibly understand how we appreciated this issue of fresh bread. The biscuits were no doubt very wholesome, but this is more than can be said of the tough ration of *trek* ox. A mincing machine was very useful, otherwise it was almost impossible to eat the meat ration. When boiled, it was very unpalatable, and we often had it in this way for breakfast before starting the day's march.

STANDING: LIEUTENANT JARVIS, LIEUTENANT DARWIN, CAPTAIN CHRISTIAN, 2ND-LIEUTENANT BROWN, 2ND-LIEUTENANT STANSFIELD. SEATED: CAPTAIN ESSON, CAPTAIN ORGAN, MAJOR FEARON, CAPTAIN FERRAR, CAPTAIN WILLIAMS. FRONT: 2ND-LIEUTENANT BUNBURY.

OFFICERS AT BLOEMFONTEIN, TAKEN A FEW DAYS AFTER ARRIVAL OF BATTALION.

On the 19th March, our division was reviewed by Lord Roberts, when he addressed every two regiments in turn. He gave us all special praise for the way we had marched, and for never losing touch of Cronje till we had him safely trapped, and to us, in particular, attached great credit for our defence of Kitchener's Kop against the determined attack of the Boers, which prevented Cronje from receiving his much-needed reinforcements, and thereby hastening his surrender.

A few days after our arrival we were joined by the Royal Warwickshire Regiment, and thus our brigade was complete.

We had not been long in Bloemfontein before enteric and dysentery made their appearance amongst the troops, the former being probably due to the bad water which had been drunk on the march, and the latter very likely to the same cause, combined with exposure. Owing to this during the months of April and May, the regiment lost about 20 men. There was a good deal of rain, and their blanket shelters afforded the troops little protection.

We had occasional reports that the enemy were in close proximity to the town, and this meant the doubling of the picquets, and once our brigade was actually ordered out, but as no signs of the Boers could be discovered, we returned to camp. They certainly were hovering round the town, for they captured the waterworks, but this put us to no great inconvenience, as there were several springs close at hand, and the town was more or less independent of the waterworks.

Every morning we had drills and exercises, and in order to keep the men fit, there was an occasional route march. By the end of March our strength in officers was increased by the arrival of Lieutenants Gunthorpe and Wardle, who had been wounded at Paardeberg, and Captain Holmes, who had arrived from home.

On the 4th April, the 18th Brigade was ordered to proceed to Springfield *kopje*, about seven miles east of Bloemfontein, the increased activity of the Boers rendering its occupation necessary. In the afternoon, just as we had arrived there, a heavy thunderstorm broke before we had time to erect our shelters. The ground was very soon converted into a quagmire, and there was no cover to be had anywhere. The Essex Regiment, who were on our flank, had one man killed by the lightning and another injured.

Here we were close to the projected line of railway to Wepener. On all sides of us, for miles, was the open, rolling *veldt*, broken on the north by an isolated *kopje*, whilst to the west lay the Bloemfontein hills. Eastwards, five or six miles off, lay a chain of *kopjes*, which had for some time been occupied by the enemy, and amusing messages, often containing a certain amount of irony, passed between their signallers and ours.

Our *kopje*, which was an extensive one, had seven posts, with a company on each, and as these were reinforced by night, the picquet duty, even when divided amongst four battalions, came round very frequently. Our bivouacs were pleasantly situated on the south side, and several trees round about afforded us a grateful shade during the heat of the day, a luxury that hitherto we had been quite unaccustomed to.

At this camp the Colonel rejoined, having recovered from his wound, and we were also glad to see many men return, for we were none too strong, one quarter of our strength having been practically struck off during the advance along the Modder, from killed and wounded alone.

On the 14th April, our Volunteer company arrived; three officers and 100 non-commissioned officers and men. They had marched from Norval's Pont, were a very fine body of men, and a welcome addition to our numbers, which before they came had been reduced to 14 officers and 655 rank and file.

This company was attached to the battalion till October, when it left with orders for home, but the unexpected turn the war took at that time, necessitated its retention in the country, for it was detained with many others before they arrived at Cape Town.

Thunderstorms were very prevalent in the Free State at this time, and the rain was almost incessant, the whole brigade being frequently swamped out of their bivouacs.

We had been told that the rainy season ended with February, but it looked as if it was then only commencing.

On the reconstruction of the field force for the advance on Pretoria, we changed our divisional number for the third and last time, and became part of the new 11th Division, in conjunction with a brigade of Guards, the latter consisting of:

The 3rd Battalion Grenadier Guards
The 1st Battalion Coldstream Guards
The 2nd Battalion Coldstream Guards
The 1st Battalion Scots Guards

under Major-General Inigo Jones, the division being commanded by Lieutenant-General R. Pole-Carew, C.B. The latter visited our brigade, and made a short speech to each regiment in turn.

On the 22nd April, we left Springfield *kop* in order to take part with the whole of our new division in an expedition, which had for its object the cutting off of the Boer force then threatening Dewetsdorp. We already knew that some *kopjes* in our line of advance were occupied by the enemy, and that we should probably have to turn them out. We handed over our tents, which had only arrived two days previously, to the 19th Brigade, which relieved us, and set out once more on the *trek*.

We had only come off outpost duty the same morning, and were, consequently, detailed as baggage guard, and thereby prevented from taking an active part in the little engagement at Leeuwkop, resulting in the retreat of the enemy from this position, which we in turn occupied the same night.

The Welsh had an officer (Captain Prothero) mortally wounded, and a few other casualties, so, too, had the Warwickshire; whilst the Essex and ourselves had not a man hit The Guards' Brigade, moving on a parallel road on our right flank, was not engaged.

We continued our march on the 23rd, and joined hands with the Guards at the junction of the Dewetsdorp-Bloemfontein roads. In the afternoon the Boers were again encountered by our advanced patrols, and the latter were fired on by the occupants of a farm flying a white flag, whose owner had given up his arms a few days before, a pass having been granted him to go in and out of Bloemfontein. We burnt the farm, and carried off all the food and forage we could find. In the afternoon of the 24th, we were again in action, and our guns opened on the Boers, who showed in considerable strength on some hills flanking our route. They bolted after about an hour's shelling, and the 18th Brigade bivouacked a few miles further on, near a farm, in the midst of an extensive plain. Several Boer wounded were found in the farm, and we also picked up two on the march. The next day the regiment formed the advanced guard, and we marched to Vaal Bank, Here we saw the movement of troops near Dewetsdorp, and opened up communication with General Rundle's column, only to find that the enemy had *trekked* in a northerly direction. On receipt of this intelligence, the cavalry went on to Thaba 'Nchu, and our division returned to Bloemfontein by a slightly different route, burning any farms that had no male occupants, whether they were flying white flags or not We reached the town, after a tiring march, on Sunday, the 29th April, having covered about seventy miles in this expedition.

Everything now pointed to a speedy advance north, the account of which must be reserved for another chapter.

CHAPTER 4

To Pretoria

The two days we spent in Bloemfontein were very busy ones. Supplies had to be made up, ammunition drawn, and warm clothing and necessaries to be issued to every man against the coming winter. During our absence no end of parcels, containing socks, shirts, handkerchiefs, mufflers, Crimean headgear, and various other articles, which had accumulated at the base during the last two months, had at last found their way up to the front They had to be stowed away somehow; or left in store, never to be seen again.

A draft of 99 men (mainly Section D) arrived just in time to take part in the advance. They were under command of Captain Orr, who had recovered from his wounds, and Lieutenants Walker and Bastow, who had arrived out from home. This addition to our ranks made us only 700 strong, as, besides casualties along the Modder River, we must have had about fifty men in hospital from enteric and other complaints.

All ranks were delighted on finding that our division was to march with the centre column, and that Lord Roberts himself was to accompany it.

On the 1st May, we set out on the long-talked-of advance to Pretoria, our first march being to Karee siding, where the fight had taken place about a month before. Karee, at this time, was as far as we had control of the railway. The sun was still very hot in the middle of the day, and continues so all throughout the South African winter, consequently the men felt this march a severe one, being unaccustomed to their serge clothing, which they were now wearing for the first time, it being a great deal warmer than the khaki drill, which had now been discarded.

We arrived at Karee shortly after dark, the baggage never turning up till the middle of the night. This often happened, in fact, it sometimes did not come in till the next morning.

Leaving Lieutenant Walker and 100 men to guard this camp temporarily, the division marched on the next afternoon to a *nek* about two miles outside the station. Here we bivouacked, and were off again at daybreak, our objective being Brandfort, a *trek* of twelve miles, the town, or rather village, as we should call it in England, lying on the other side of the broad plain that stretched before us.

Four of our companies formed the left flank guard to the division. As we approached the town, the guns opened fire on the enemy, who were holding the adjoining hills. We presently heard the well-known *pic-poc* of the Mausers, which did not, however, last long, and the division marched in, neither brigade having fired a shot.

We remained all next day at Brandfort, where we were joined by 2nd-Lieutenant Morgan, on appointment The delay was caused by finding the bridge over the *spruit* blown up by the retreating Boers, and it was necessary to repair it before supplies could be brought up for the army.

On the 3rd, Captain Maitland (reserve of officers) arrived with a draft of 94 men. We were now very strong in officers, and the mess president began to wear a worried look, as he saw the space on the officers' wagon becoming more and more limited, owing to the extra kits that had to be put on it.

It was not very long before the little bridge at Brandfort was repaired, and the morning of the 4th saw us on the move once more, the battalion forming the advance guard. We halted for about a couple of hours to reconnoitre, and very shortly learned that the enemy were in position at the Vet River. So on we went, and our field and naval guns both opened fire at about 3 p.m. The Boers at once replied with what appeared to be three or four guns, but it was difficult to say how many they had. Both sides kept up a continuous fire till dark, the Boers warming to their work during the last hour. They made very good shooting, and had by far the best target, for our guns, as well as ourselves, were bang in the open, whereas they were well concealed.

Their shells did little or no damage, and our volunteer company, who were up in line with the guns, had no casualties. They kept pitching right amongst the leading companies of the regiment, but as they did not burst effectively, no harm was done. Had a few been correctly fused, we must have had a very warm time of it. One of our volunteers thus related his experience of this shell fire:

We were the advance guard, and our company was right in front, supporting the artillery. Here we had what proved to be, thank God, nothing worse than a very nerve-trying experience. For two hours and a half we lay prone under shell fire. There were some narrow escapes, and if the shells had burst in the air instead of on the ground, as most of them did, we should have been riddled. One burst two feet off Corporal ——, and, serious as it was, we could not help laughing at the way he moved off. The nearest to me burst about six yards in front of me, and spattered me with earth. I have a bullet from it As we could almost tell from the sound when each was coming, there was some ducking of heads. It was grand to see the cool way the gunners worked, just crouching down as each shell came their way. Just before the end of the fight, we were told off to take the position on the left, and the Guards on the right I had received instructions from the Captain as to my section; but we got no order to advance before dark, so we retired a few hundred yards and bivouacked for the night Our artillery—we had field, naval and garrison— shelled the enemy out of their position before we retired. Contrary to my expectations, I had no feeling of fear exactly, a quickened beating of the heart, some excitement, wondering where the next shell would fall, and what people at home at that particular moment were doing, was what I noted most

As the enemy showed no inclination to vacate their position, General Pole-Carew determined to force the attack, and directed the Guards to assault the *kopjes* in front, whilst the Green Howards, supported by the Warwickshire, were to work round on the left We were just on the point of moving off with this object, when a message came, countermanding the order. No doubt this attack was just what the Boers were praying for, and though we should probably have taken the position, nothing would have been gained by it, except a long casualty roll. Next morning, expecting to have a fight, we found that the Boers had *trekked* off in the night, after destroying the railway bridge (a five-span one) over the river. As the banks were thirty feet high, and the *drift* very difficult to negotiate, it took the headquarter and divisional baggage all day long to cross. Half the regiment was on duty with drag-ropes on the far bank, from 4 p.m. to 8.30, helping to get the heavy wagons up the steep slope, after which they marched in by moonlight to the bivouac, some five miles further on.

On the 7th we only did three miles, and this was to Smaldeel junction, where the Winburg and Pretoria lines meet, and there we remained all day, never expecting that the 8th would prove a day of rest as well. On the 9th, we started again, and reached Welgelegen siding, a good march of eighteen miles. We always kept close to the railway; in fact, during the remainder of the campaign, we were never at any time very far distant from it The 10th found us again doing advance guard, our intelligence giving us the prospect of a fight at the well-known Zand River, of convention fame, where the enemy was supposed to be in force, but it was the same story again, for after hurriedly exchanging some shots with our advanced troops, they made off, after blowing up the bridge on their way.

Away to our right we could hear firing going on, telling us that General Tucker, with his division (the 7th), was engaged, and on the left the Inniskilling Dragoons were having some fighting, losing two officers and many men.

We halted for a time on the far bank of the river, and, pushing on, we reached Riet *spruit*, after a tiresome march of eighteen miles, through numerous patches of *mealie* fields. Here we bivouacked, and on the 11th halted at Geneva siding, a good twenty miles further on. Steyn, we heard, was at Kroonstadt, which he had now made the Free State capital, and was busy drawing up encouraging manifestoes for his flying *burghers*. Being told of what splendid defensive positions barred the way to the town, we really thought there would be some show of resistance. It was only show, and nothing more, for many trenches had been dug and positions prepared, but no one seemed inclined to stop and occupy them.

Starting at the usual hour of 6 a.m., we reached the outskirts of Kroonstadt by noon, but it was not till 5 p.m., after considerable delay, that we gained our bivouac on the north side of the town. Lord Roberts and his staff were drawn up near the market place to see the division march in. Shortly after our arrival, the following brigade order was published:

> The G.O.C. the brigade has been directed to convey to all ranks under his command the special gratification of the field-marshal, commanding-in-chief, at the splendid marching powers and plucky endurance shown by them during the past twelve days.

Kroonstadt seemed a poor sort of place, very similar to Bloemfontein, but on a much smaller scale. The surroundings are prettier than those of the capital, the banks of the River Valsch being well lined with trees, which are so rare in the Free State.

Here we were forced to remain for eight days, as the fine bridge over the river had been blown up, and the different regiments were employed day and night, by four-hour shifts, in cutting a deviation for the line, which, in order to avoid the steepness of the banks, had to make a considerable detour. There was a full moon, and the work progressed by night almost as fast as it did by day.

The 4th Battalion Mounted Infantry were in bivouac on the other side of the river. They had accompanied us all the way along the Modder, and had had their share of the fighting, but till now we had seen very little of them. Lieutenant Stansfeld and twenty men left us here to join them, as they were short of officers.

We had a very easy time of it at Kroonstadt, for with the exception of an occasional picquet and a turn at the deviation, there was nothing at all to do, and everyone had time to go to the town to look for any necessaries he needed; only a limited supply of food was procurable, and this was speedily bought up.

We were quite glad to start again on the 22nd, and a 20-mile march brought us to Honingspruit, where we arrived just before dark, having only set out at 8 a.m., owing to the late arrival of our rations for the day. It is difficult to describe the intense monotony of a day's march in the Free State. You plod along, mile after mile, with nothing to break the unvarying scenery, if it can be called such, of the "illimitable *veldt*," which at times seems almost as expansive as the open sea. We felt that the Boers did not mean to fight, so that we were even without this hope to cheer our spirits.

The advanced companies had generally with them a motley collection of lurchers, terriers and curs of high and low degree, and their occasional courses after the hares, which were continually kicked up by the men, might be counted as amongst the most interesting events of the day. The hares, if they broke straight away in front, generally managed to escape, but sometimes they doubled back amongst the advancing regiments and were knocked over by some lucky soldier, whom they happened, in their desperation, to run against.

The usual story was being circulated that the Boers were going to show fight soon, and that they were strongly entrenched at the Rhenoster River. This was our next halting place, fourteen miles distant, but when we arrived there, all we found were some rifle pits neatly cut in the river bank, and the bridge over the deep *drift* completely destroyed. The rails were also torn up for a considerable distance, and were thrown up at intervals of one hundred yards, all bent and twisted, by frequent charges of dynamite.

On the 24th we reached Vredeport, fourteen miles further on, and on the next day Grootvlei, about the same distance. Both of these places were simply stations on the line, with not another building anywhere near for miles. As we marched along we noticed on all sides large tracts of burning *veldt*, which had probably been set on fire either by the Boers or by our mounted troops. Owing to there being little or no rain in the Free State and Transvaal in the winter, the grass soon becomes withered and dry. A lighted match, dropped carelessly upon it, will set thousands of acres on fire, making the charred debris very disagreeable to march through, because of the fine black dust, and spoiling for the infantry, toiling along in the rear, many a comfortable camping ground. Often on our arrival at our bivouac, we looked much more like a battalion of stokers, owing to our blackened clothes and faces, than a regiment of Her Majesty's Line.

Some of us reasoned that the Transvaal Boers, once they got through the Free State, would stop and defend their own territory at the River Vaal, and that an obstinate resistance would be offered us there, as well as at Pretoria, which we were told was mined all round, and, with its forts, would be a very hard nut to crack. On our arrival at Taaibosch *spruit*, six miles from the river, we heard that they had all decamped, and that we were to encounter no opposition on entering the Transvaal.

The battalion was detailed for baggage and rearguard the day we crossed the Vaal (May 27th), and the baggage companies waded through the river at the *drift*, whilst those composing the rearguard crossed a few hundred yards higher up by means of a pulley bridge, where the river was deeper.

Vereeniging, the town we now reached, was merely a collection of the everlasting corrugated iron huts that you meet with so often in South Africa. Several coal shafts, dotted here and there, had quite a homely look for some of our mining community, who were busy comparing them to those in Bradford, Pudsey and other towns in the Yorkshire coal districts. On the outskirts were traces of recent Boer camps, and we were glad to see that several culverts on the line had not been interfered with. We found afterwards that no damage had been done to the railway running from here to Pretoria. The cause of this probably was that the Free State railway, which had been torn up and damaged in every conceivable way, belonged to that State, and was heavily in debt to the Cape government, while the Transvaal railway belonged to the Netherlands Company, and so was left alone, many of the Transvaalers themselves having shares in it

On the 28th May, we reached Klip River, a long march of twenty-two miles, over the burnt *veldt*, arriving at our bivouac in the evening very tired, very dirty, and, worse still, very hungry, for the rations that day only consisted of a quarter of a pound of flour, in addition to the usual quantity of fresh tough *trek* ox. It was very seldom that we ever got a ration of preserved *bully* beef, and when we did, we considered it a great luxury. The keen air of the high *veldt* made everyone develop an extraordinary appetite, and though the usual allowance of five biscuits, weighing about a pound, and a similar quantity of fresh meat, may seem enough to satisfy one, yet there were very few men of the battalion who did not turn in for the night without feeling hungry. It was getting bitterly cold now at sundown, and the next morning Major Ferguson's thermometer registered 16 degrees of frost; all the water had a thick coating of ice, and, in consequence, our morning wash was a bit sketchy.

The next day proved a long one. We made a bad start by having to cross the railway bridge in single file, which, for a division, was a tedious process. Then at the *drift* one of the naval guns broke down the dilapidated bridge, and none of us saw a blanket or greatcoat till 3 o'clock next morning.

Johannesburg, the Golden City, was sighted at 11 a.m., and there, in front of us, lay the famous gold reef, extending for fourteen miles east and west, with its numerous chimneys and shafts, and huge heaps of tailings of a peculiar light grey colour.

We were marching right along the line on Elandsfontein, and as we got closer up we heard again the well-known *pop* of the Mauser, and saw the mounted infantry gallop up the slope towards the town. Most of these happened to be our own M.I. company, and the battalion to which they belonged got specially thanked in orders for the work they did in seizing the station at Germiston, and stopping two trains that were on the point of departing north. Lieutenants Stansfeld and Nevile both took an active part in this affair.

On arrival outside Elandsfontein, our volunteer company, under Captain Bell, was sent as a guard to the Simmer and Jack mine at the request of the manager, which turned out to be a very agreeable experience for them. They were supplied with tea, coffee and biscuits, and those not actually on sentry were able to make use of the billiard and reading rooms. They certainly fared better than their comrades in the open, who did not get their blankets till the early morning.

The next day the 7th Division, which had been operating on our left, marched through Johannesburg, which had surrendered peaceably, and bivouacked on the high ground northwest of the town. Our division was ordered to parade for a march through the streets, for the purpose of hoisting the British Flag, but this was afterwards cancelled, and we remained where we were for the day. This function, however, took place on the 31st, the 18th Brigade being at the head of the troops on their march through the town.

The square where the Union Jack was hoisted was so confined, that there was only space for two battalions. The usual formalities were, however, observed, three cheers being given for the Queen, but, unfortunately, there was no band to play the national anthem. The men were very heartily received by the populace, who freely distributed amongst them oranges, tobacco and bread, and in some cases, even money was scattered amongst the ranks. It is a wonderful town, considering the few years (fifteen) that it has been in existence, and the new appearance of the buildings gave one the idea that it had certainly been run up very quickly. There was much excitement amongst the black population at our arrival, who evidently appreciated the prospect of a change of masters. They kept on shouting, "God bless Queen Victoria!" and "Damn Boers!"

We marched on through the town, past Orange Grove, and thought we would never get to our bivouac, nor did we reach it till nearly ten o'clock, and then discovered, to our dismay, that we had halted close to a hospital for lepers and small-pox patients. Imagine our horror later at finding we had all been drinking the water from a stream in which the patients' clothes had been washed a short time previously, but as far as one could tell, there were no ill-effects afterwards. The doctors of the hospital were very kind, offering us beds and food, the former of which some of us accepted, as well as the food, on it being explained that the ward had not been occupied for some years. Our bivouac was about seven miles outside the town, and most of the officers and a few non-commissioned officers were allowed to walk or drive there, to experience the luxury of sitting down in front of a tablecloth once more, to say nothing of a square meal.

We remained at this camp till the 3rd June, when we *trekked* for Rietfontein, eight miles off, and the next day, at 10 a.m., found us at Six-Mile *spruit*, about seven miles further on, just outside Pretoria. Heavy firing was going on in our front, and we took up a position in extended order behind a low-lying hill, where we remained for a couple of hours, not under a very heavy fire, but there were quite enough bullets kicking up the dust to make things a bit lively for us.

There was fighting going on on our left front, and shells kept dropping on our right, evidently aimed at the naval guns, which had already come into action. Many of the enemy's shells went high, and pitched amongst the ambulances in our rear, and one went precious near the balloon, which was anchored some way behind us.

At about 3 o'clock, we were ordered to continue our advance on Pretoria, now only four miles distant As we marched on we came under some desultory fire from a hill about 1,800 yards off, on our left This delayed us somewhat, and darkness coming on, we were obliged to bivouac where we were for the night. We had only one man wounded in the regiment, and the Welsh and Essex also came off very lightly, and so would the Warwickshire, had it not been for the premature explosion of a shell from one of the naval guns, which killed one man, and wounded about a dozen others. These guns made good practice at two of the forts outside the town, and as there was no reply from them, we concluded that they were unoccupied, which afterwards proved true. Next morning, shortly after dawn, we heard great bursts of cheering, and very soon learnt that the town had surrendered unconditionally.

Some sniping went on for some time after, and the battalion was ordered to occupy a *kopje* near the station, from which we were withdrawn a couple of hours later. We were then formed up to march through the town at 1 o'clock, but it was not till well on in the afternoon that we moved off, and proceeded to the Grand Square, where Lord Roberts and his escort were drawn up close to the Dutch Church, waiting to see us go by. We marched through the square at the head of our brigade in column of sections, the balconies of the hotels and principal houses being thronged with spectators, many of whom cheered each battalion as it entered the saluting ground.

On our way to our bivouac, two miles on the west side of the town, we passed by Kruger's house, which we quickly recognised by the two white lions guarding its portals. Mrs. Kruger still occupied the house, a most unpretentious one, over which was an officers' guard of the King's Own Scottish Borderers.

Now as to the President himself. He had fled eastwards at the last moment, taking with him many of his prisoners and a considerable amount of his country's gold, determined, it was said to make a final stand in the Lydenberg mountains, and we soon realised that Pretoria was not our final goal, but that there was still more marching and fighting, cold nights and short rations in store for us.

CHAPTER 5

The Advance Eastwards

We expected to remain at Pretoria for two or three days at least, and were rather disappointed at getting orders at 10 a.m. on the 7th June, to move at noon to Silverton, a little station ten miles away, on the Delagoa Bay line.

Before leaving, we had been joined by Lieutenant Walker and 2nd-Lieutenant Sanderson, so now mustered 22 officers. On our way, and just outside Pretoria, we saw most of the prisoners taken by the Boers during the war, drawn up by companies near the racecourse. There were in all 158 officers and 3,029 men, but about 900 more officers and men were made to accompany the Boers in their retreat eastwards. Amongst the former we found three of our own men, who had been returned as missing at Paardeberg. It appears they had gone down to the Modder after dark for a drink, and not being able to find their way back, they had spent the night with a picquet of the Gloucestershire Regiment In the morning, in trying to find their own lines, they had knocked up against a party of Boers who had come out from Kitchener's Kop, and being outnumbered, were taken prisoners.

We heard that the enemy had been sniping our cavalry patrols near Silverton, and it was later reported that they were in force in a strong position running north and south of the railway, and about 20 miles east of Pretoria, which accounted for our sudden move on the 7th.

Pretoria is surrounded by hills, and is a well-wooded, prettily-situated town, somewhat larger in extent than Bloemfontein. The public buildings are large and imposing, notably the Volksraad and the Artillery Barracks.

The streets are broad and well-lit up by electricity, and are kept clean and well watered. It was certainly the most attractive-looking town in either republic that we had as yet come across.

Our division remained for three days at Silverton, and on the 11th moved off five miles in a south-easterly direction, to take part in the operation of driving the Boers from their new position. The action commenced the same day, and lasted till the 13th, when the enemy were driven off, the cavalry bearing the brunt of the fighting, losing Lord Airlie, commanding 12th Lancers, killed, and many officers and men. Our brigade, in fact the division, did not come in for any serious fighting in this engagement, which was afterwards known as the battle of Diamond Hill.

We marched back to Pretoria on the 15th, and on the way, just as we had passed Silverton, the whole brigade was brought to a standstill by an excited engine-driver, who, rushing through the trees from the direction of the railway, shouted and screamed to us to send reinforcements, as the enemy were at Eerste Fabriken, the next station. On being questioned, he said that there were a lot of Boers there, and that he could take two companies in his train straightaway. We hardly credited his story; but some mounted infantry men were, however, sent back to reconnoitre, and found that the alarm was caused by two or three sportsmen who were shooting in the neighbourhood.

We made our bivouac two miles east of Pretoria, close to the railway, and remained there quietly till the 21st June, when we took to the road again, and marching over much the same ground as on the 15th, drew up for the night at Marks' farm, about a mile beyond Eerste Fabriken. Mr. Marks was the owner of a large distillery at this place, and though his whiskey was not very good, we were very glad to get it. We certainly wanted something that night to cheer us up, for it rained in torrents, and the three companies on outpost duty had but a sorry time of it.

After this our division was split up, the Guards' Brigade *trekking* off about four miles to their right, whilst we and the Royal Warwickshire were despatched to picquet the hills near Frankpoort (or Edendale), where we were joined by the 85th Field Battery and two naval 12-pounders. The other two battalions of our brigade remained in the vicinity of Eerste Fabriken.

Whilst in this camp our mounted infantry, which were at Peinaar's Poort, had several brushes with the Boers, and near us several colonial mounted infantry men had been killed when on patrol duty. We had a good deal of picquet work, there were many alarms, and standing to arms in the bitter cold of the slowly dawning day was part of the usual programme.

Dawn appeared to be the coldest time of day in South Africa, and this "standing by" for an hour before daylight, when the frost was on the ground, was miserable work, till at length the welcome sun came peeping over the outpost hill at 7.30, when everyone soon got warm again and forgot their troubles.

When we arrived at Edendale we had been without any mails for six weeks, owing to the cutting of our communications time after time by De Wet and other Boer leaders. In the end we got them all except one (that of May 3rd), and since then, during the rest of the war they always turned up fairly regularly, with the exception of one in December, 1900, which was taken from a wrecked train on the Delagoa Bay line. We, however, never got half our parcels during the first year of the campaign, as they were all kept back down country, and later on were looted.

We were over a month altogether at Edendale, and were there served out with British "warm" coats of the Indian pattern, which were a welcome addition to many of the men's kits, especially those who had lost their greatcoats between Paardeberg and Bloemfontein. We also got the long-expected, long-delayed "Queen's Chocolate" but none the less welcome on that account. Most of the men sent it home to their relatives or friends for safe keeping.

Captain Holmes now left us for the mounted infantry, taking over the command of the Green Howards' company, *vice* Major Handcock, who had been appointed to the command of the battalion. Major Cotesworth, from home, joined us about the same time, taking over Captain Holmes' company.

Not many days before we left we received a large supply of corrugated iron, which had been sent over from our prisoners' quarters at Waterval, and we were kept busy making this into huts, which were a great protection against the cold.

During our four weeks' sojourn at Edendale we amused ourselves by having several football matches, and General Stephenson and staff, who occupied a farmhouse near our camp, generally joined in these games. The general also organised a gymkhana, which took place on the 14th July, proving a great success, as there were lots of entries from the brigade.

In the bending race, Lieutenant Stansfeld was first out of forty competitors, and Captain Holmes second in the tandem race, whilst C company won the calf in the looting race, the most coveted prize of all. We had an occasional day's leave to Pretoria, a privilege which was granted to all officers. The train journey from Eerste Fabriken was rather a jumpy business, especially the return one, and we all had to take any seat we could find in the open trucks, and often found ourselves sitting perched up on flour bags, ammunition boxes, or bread for the troops. It was not very long before the eatables in Pretoria became exhausted, and it was difficult to get jam or bread, or, in fact, provisions of any kind, except, perhaps, some smoked articles of German manufacture, which were not very inviting.

At last our welcome orders came, and on 23rd July we *trekked* off, the Warwickshire leading, the battery and naval guns following. We reached Elands River station, about ten miles distant, in the afternoon, the Welsh and Essex moving on the right of the railway and we on the left. Away still further on the right, was the Guards' Brigade, and we did not actually meet them till they passed us at Bronkhorst *spruit* We bivouacked close beside the stream on anything but a choice piece of ground, it being very wet and boggy, and a few more nights of it would probably have given us all aches and pains for the rest of our lives. So we were glad to start off on the morrow to Bronkhorst *spruit* station, which we reached early in the afternoon, an eight-mile march.

We bivouacked near the station and *spruit*, the latter quite worthy of the name of river in the Transvaal. The bridge over it was found to be badly damaged, and the Welsh were left to make a deviation, as well as to guard the line in the neighbourhood. The remainder of our brigade continued their march, skirting the *spruit* in a southerly direction for about three miles, before coming to the high road to Pretoria. Here there was some delay, as the *drift* over the *spruit* was a bad one, and the wagons took some time in getting over it. The baggage of the mounted troops was all going along the main road, so our brigade struck a track a little to the south of it, in order to avoid congestion. We here passed close to the graves of the ill-fated 94th Regiment, which called to mind that unfortunate episode in the last Boer war, twenty years before.

A short march of eight miles, took us to the Wilge River, where we were joined by the Guards' Brigade, but they continued their march a few hours later, whilst we and the Warwickshire remained near the *drift*, three or four miles from Wilge station.

In the afternoon the sky became overcast, and rain fell heavily, and continued without intermission till well into the next morning. It was a regular Transvaal storm, but it, fortunately, only skirted our halting place, so that we did not get the full benefit of it, though the night we spent was a hard one to beat for discomfort. This was, to a great extent, caused by many of our blankets and greatcoats not having turned up, owing to the transport having for a time lost its way. This storm broke right over the Essex Regiment, who had halted about a mile in our rear, and they presented a very woebegone appearance when they joined us next morning.

Ever since our start from Bloemfontein we had discarded, as sleeping accommodation, the old Boer shelter picked up at Klip *drift*, owing to the large number of officers now with the battalion. Most of us by this time used a small *tente d'abri*, and as for the men, they got very handy in rigging up their blankets so as to form a very good protection against both sun and rain.

The next day we made a late start, but as we had only six miles to march, it did not matter, and we were at our bivouac before dark. We were delayed by a small *spruit*, as a bridge had to be made by the sappers in order to get the baggage across.

The Essex were ordered to proceed to Wilge River station to help to make the deviation at the bridge which had been wrecked, whilst we and the Warwickshire remained for the night at Bosman's *kraal*, and went on to Balmoral, a little station on the line, where we arrived on the 27th July.

As we had to stay here for three weeks, we were very fortunate in the site chosen for our camp, which was in a farm studded with huge eucalyptus trees, affording us a pleasant shade. There was a plentiful supply of good water, which ran close by the cook-house, and arrangements were made for the men to have a bath whenever they liked. This was preferable to being dumped down on the open *veldt*.

We had two companies daily on picquet, one on a hill in rear of our camp, and the other over the trenches, which we made on our left flank. We also had to furnish escorts from time to time for the convoys between Wilge River and Brugspruit, ten miles east of us, where the Grenadiers had halted, the remainder of their brigade having gone on to Oliphant's River and Middleburg, the latter place being as far as the railway was open.

At Balmoral we were joined by a section of our mounted infantry, under Lieutenant Nevile, and later on by the whole company, under Captain Holmes. One of their men, Private Varlow, was killed on the 12th August whilst patrolling a few miles north of the line.

By the middle of August, all the deviations rendered necessary by the broken bridges had been completed, and sufficient supplies had

TRENCHES AT BALMORAL

BALMORAL

been collected for another forward movement. We, consequently, got orders on the 15th to march to Brugspruit and relieve the Grenadiers, who departed for Middleburg the next morning. We sent two companies, E and F, under Major Cotesworth, to Witbank colliery, five miles up the line, and another went on picquet at Howard's colliery, two miles north. On the 18th, three companies, F, H and G, and the volunteers, under Major Fearon, were ordered to Middleburg, as escort to a huge convoy, a long march of over twenty miles, and on the 20th they were followed as far as Oliphant's River by the remainder of the regiment on their relief by the Buffs.

In the meantime, the rest of our brigade was following us up, being relieved along the line by other corps as they advanced. Marching on to Pan by half-battalions, we finally arrived at Wonderfontein on the 23rd.

Middleburg, which we passed through, seemed a pretty little town, and was evidently, from its situation and the numerous farms in the neighbourhood, an important trades centre in this part of the Transvaal. The outskirts where we bivouacked had been very much cut up by the constant passing of mounted troops, and the dust there forcibly reminded us of the days we spent at De Aar.

The country which we now passed through was exactly similar to that traversed in the Free State during the past seven months. In fact, if anything, it seemed still more desolate, and the constant tracts of blackened *veldt* made marching anything but pleasant, especially for the companies in the rear, who got the full benefit of the kicked-up ashes. The farms along our route were few and far between, and all were unoccupied.

On our arrival at Wonderfontein, we found that the rest of our division had already assembled there. On the 24th, a short march of about seven miles brought us outside Belfast, where we were detached from our brigade, and ordered to hold a hill opposite the extreme right of the Boers, who were barring our advance in a strong position, about ten miles in extent, running north and south of Belfast We attacked the next day, our division being near the town, whilst General French, with the mounted troops, made a turning movement on the left flank. General Buller was opposed to the enemy's left and centre.

An exchange of artillery fire was the chief feature of the three days' fighting which followed, but on the 26th General Bulla: successfully pressed his attack, with the result that the enemy were scattered in all directions, leaving a great number of dead and wounded in our hands. Our divisional loss was trifling, being only thirty-eight killed and wounded, and out of these only seven belonged to the 18th Brigade. Our mounted infantry took a leading part in this fight, having one officer (Lieutenant Tarbet) and five men wounded.

The 2nd Battalion Rifle Brigade lost about twenty killed, including three officers, and many wounded, in an attack on a farm at Bergendal, which was most obstinately held by the enemy.

Belfast seemed a poor sort of place, with the usual widely-dispersed galvanised iron huts. It owes its existence chiefly to its coal mines, which no doubt will one day become valuable.

On the 28th August, the 18th Brigade left Belfast, its destination being Swartz *kopje*, about ten miles north, amongst the mountains. The scenery now became less monotonous as we advanced. Our brigade was strung out all along the line of march as escort to the baggage, and had hard work getting some of the wagons up the steep slopes.

Our first halt for the night was not at a very inviting spot, as there was no water for the tired men or horses, except what could be got by digging, and that was of a very muddy nature.

After this, we turned south and marched down the hills, reaching a small plain a few miles north of Machadodorp, where the road crossed the one leading to Lydenberg. This spot is known as Helvetia. The scenery around, to some extent, resembles that of Switzerland, and in Waterval-boven you can see the exact model of a sealed pattern Swiss village. Here we joined hands with some of General Buller's troops, under command of Major-General Lyttleton.

This force departed for Lydenberg the next day, and we, after remaining at Helvetia till the 6th September, got orders to send the headquarters and five companies to Waterval-onder. There is a very steep gradient in the line from Waterval-boven to Onder, necessitating a cog-wheel track, which, luckily, the Boers had not destroyed, but they had removed all the engines with the cog-wheel machinery. This was rather a nuisance, as only a couple of trucks could be used in one journey.

At Boven we met with a great windfall. In a large store near the station was found a quantity of groceries and tinned food, and what was perhaps more appreciated, some whiskey and claret This was taken over by the Army Service Corps, and issued to the different regiments simply for the asking. We sent down an ambulance, and filled it with tea, coffee, tinned butter, preserved soup, Quaker oats, and all sorts of things, which well replenished our worn-out larder.

PRISONERS AT SPRINGS

MAKING THE DEVIATION BRIDGE AT KAAPMUIDEN

On the 12th September we marched along the line to Nooigedacht, in company with the Essex, the Warwickshire and Welsh having been left at Boven and Onder respectively. In our progress we descended about 1,000 feet, and we at once remarked on the change in the vegetation, for we now everywhere came across semi-tropical flowers and plants of various kinds. It was a great relief, after the uninteresting character of the *veldt*, to see some variety in this way.

Passing by Nooigedacht, we noticed the barbed wire enclosure in which the Boers had confined their prisoners. They had been in the open all the time they were there, and every conceivable kind of shelter, made of sods and rags, had been erected to protect them from the sun, which in this valley is very hot in the middle of the day all the year round. Seven officers and 1,800 men had been released by General Buller on the 30th August, and only a few, chiefly officers, had been taken, on to Barberton.

On the 13th we reached the Godwaan River, where we chose a nice spot for our bivouac, close to the stream which here joins the Crocodile, and many of us revelled in the luxury of a bathe. The road, which up to now ran along the railway, here breaks off, and in order to get to our destination, Nelspruit, we had to diverge in a south-easterly direction over the mountains. Still keeping with the Essex, we started the ascent on the 14th, a good climb of 1,900 feet Getting the transport up was attended with considerable difficulty, for often double teams had to be *inspanned*, and man-handling was also necessary.

All our regimental baggage was up, however, an hour after dark, though lots of other transport were going all through the night, which, for us, was not a very pleasant one, being made still worse by the presence of some dead horses, which were lying close to our bivouac.

We had now reached the De Kaap goldfields, and there were mines all round. From the top of the cliffs on our way to the Devil's Kantoor, a splendid view opened itself to us, and the country for fifty miles round could be clearly seen. It is said to be the finest view in South Africa.

During our next day's *trek* the road got worse and worse, and just before we halted for the night most of the wagons had to be unloaded and their contents carried by the men to the top of the next rise.

Next day, the 17th, the right half-battalion was sent off with four guns to occupy Nelspruit, the remainder of the regiment following with the baggage, whilst the Essex brought up the rear. The advanced guard entered the station at about 1 p.m., and took possession of the place, all the Boers having gone a day or two before. We found six engines and about seventy trucks, but most of the latter were smashed up by having been run down an incline, while the engines had been put out of gear. There were also the charred portions of several gun carriages.

We separated from the Guards' Brigade at the top of the mountain, as they had orders to march to Avoca, and they eventually reached Komati Poort, *via* Kaapmuiden, a few days later. Kruger had arrived at Lorenzo Marques on the 11th September, after resigning the so-called reins of government to Schalk Burgher. General French had entered Barberton on the 13th September, releasing there 82 prisoners, of whom 23 were officers, and again the war was supposed to be finished.

The march into Nelspruit was the last one performed by the Green Howards as a battalion. From the commencement they had *trekked* in all about 1,000 miles; the excitement of the campaign was over, and they now had to settle down to eighteen weary months of blockhouse and picquet duty, so it was well that they could not forecast the future.

Chapter 6
The Crocodile Valley

We settled down to our work at Nelspruit, and spent the time digging trenches round the camp, fixing our defence posts, and fortifying the place generally. The day after our arrival Lord Roberts and half a battalion of the Argyll and Sutherland Highlanders arrived. The Field-Marshal, after inspecting the station, returned the next day to Pretoria, and the Highlanders left a few days afterwards. The Essex sent detachments to Crocodile Poort, Alkmaar and Elandshoek, whilst we remained at Nelspruit with General Stephenson, who made his headquarters there.

The river, which flowed about a mile from our lines, was a great treat to us. We used to bathe in it every day, there being some good pools where we could have a dive and a short swim. Unfortunately, two men (Corporal Bailey and Private Purvis) were accidentally drowned one day. Purvis had won the Distinguished Conduct Medal in the Tirah campaign. We discovered, hidden away near the river, boxes upon boxes of matches, and any amount of mottled soap, both of which were much prized.

On the 29th September, F, G and H companies and the volunteers left by rail, under Major Fearon, for Kaapmuiden, to help in cutting the deviation over the Kaap River, the three-span bridge, like so many others, having been destroyed by dynamite. When the deviation and the temporary bridge were finished, several officers got permission to go down to Komati Poort to buy stores, and to have a look round the place.

Our mounted infantry company was there, and happened to be the first troops to cross the bridge into Portuguese territory.

This bridge was a very fine one, and had been mined, and wires were laid ready for its destruction by the retreating Boers, but thanks to the efforts of the governor-general, they were induced not to sacrifice this valuable structure, the destruction of which would have crippled the trade of Delagoa Bay for months afterwards. Three miles from the bridge, you find yourself at Resaño Garcia, the little frontier station, where there was a mounted infantry picquet. Evidence of the Boers' demoralisation lay all along the line, and could not have been better exemplified. The whole place was simply littered with burnt ammunition, rifles, saddles, bags of flour and other stores. Several of their guns had been thrown into the river at Hectorspruit, where they were afterwards found.

There was no end of rolling stock at Komati, but many of the carriages had been burnt; it extended right away up the Selati railway for several miles. Every here and there the rails had been taken up so as to delay as much as possible the removal of the carriages.

There were at this time a great many accidents on the line, mainly owing to bad driving. This, of course, could not well be avoided, many of the engine drivers being mere amateurs, picked up from the different regiments, and as the line, owing to the steep gradients required really expert men, travelling on the Imperial Military Railway (as it was called) was not unattended without a considerable amount of risk.

A very bad accident occurred at Kaapmuiden shortly after the bridge was open. A train had gone down the deviation at about forty miles an hour instead of five, the result being that the engine ran off the line on the far side of the bridge, the carriages immediately in rear of it being completely telescoped, and several others derailed. The train had on board a section of the 66th Battery, of which four drivers were killed, whilst an officer and seventeen men were injured. In addition, many natives were hurt, and twenty horses were either killed outright or had to be shot

Our volunteer company left us on the 10th October, with the idea that they were returning home, as everything now wore a most peaceful aspect, but the different complexion that the war suddenly took obliged them to remain, and they were detained for some months longer in the Orange River Colony.

Perhaps they had not got as much fighting as they may have wished, yet their experiences had been many and varied. They had covered 700 miles with the regiment, and had shown us that they were not the least bit behind in marching with the best of us.

The climate of the Crocodile valley is a peculiar one, neither horses nor cattle being able to live in it except during the winter months.

RAILWAY ACCIDENT, KAAPMUIDEN

Malaria is rife, and our men were constantly falling victims to it. We had to send all our transport animals to the high *veldt* at Kaapsche Hoop in charge of Lieutenant Darwin, who was now attached to the Army Service Corps, and graded as a staff captain.

Early in October the Essex Regiment left the valley with orders for India, but, like the volunteers and many other corps with similar orders, they remained in the country for many months afterwards.

This necessitated a change in our detachments, and on our three companies being withdrawn from Kaapmuiden we held the line from Belmont Bridge to Crocodile Poort, C and E being at Belmont under Major Cotesworth, A and D at Alkmaar under Captain Orr, F and G at Crocodile Poort with Major Fearon, and the remainder with headquarters at Nelspruit

Nelspruit had been left in a most insanitary state by the Boers. Under every tree, within half-a-mile of the station, there were empty tins of all kinds, probably part of their spoil from the store at Waterval-boven. Evidently they were particularly partial to tinned herrings and tomato sauce. Filth and offal were strewn about all over the place, and it took us days to get the place clean.

Those of us who had guns and cartridges got some partridge shooting, and we now and then secured a buck, which made a welcome change in our rations.

There was also some good fishing in the river, and barbel, weighing several pounds, were often caught. As for the Boer, we never saw him. He had not quite got into working order, and we had very little experience of him whilst in the Crocodile valley. It was bad going for his horses, and he had evidently no wish to contract a go of malaria.

At this time Lieutenant Liddon and thirty men left the battalion to join the 4th M.I.

On the 23rd November we had another change, the headquarters and four companies going to Komati Poort, relieving the Royal Scots, who in turn relieved the Welsh at Barberton, the latter regiment taking our place at Nelspruit and other places we held. Captain Orr, with his company, went to Hectorspruit, whilst A, C and E, under Major Cotesworth, occupied Kaapmuiden.

Shortly after their arrival at Komati the companies there went into huts on the Lebombo Hills, close to the Portuguese frontier. Whilst at Kaapmuiden we once more revelled in the luxury of tents, having the Indian E.P. pattern, ten men in each. They were much cooler than the corrugated iron huts with wooden lining that we had at this station a few months later, for you could take down the walls at any time, and so let a free current of air pass through the tent.

The bush was very thick at Kaapmuiden, and a good deal of labour was necessary to clear the ground for our encampment. The men were also kept busy making fortified posts round the station, but were spared from trench digging as much as possible, as we found this work was conducive to fever, and so it was generally performed by natives. Later on, the whole encampment was surrounded by a strong fence of barbed wire.

In the meantime, the Boers had become more daring, and on the 7th December had come down on the railway, half-way between Alkmaar and Nelspruit, and derailed a train there. Fortunately, it was a down one, and only had on board a few sheep as rations for the troops. This must have been a great disappointment to the enemy, as no end of trains were passing up daily from Lorenzo Marques, packed as full as they could hold with stores of every description.

This derailed train was kept under fire by the Boers for several days, but when our mounted infantry arrived from Kaapsche Hoop they had all decamped. Simultaneously with this raid on the train, an attack was made on a small post six miles outside Barberton, which was held by some mounted infantry, several of them being killed and wounded, and others captured.

By the end of the year the whole regiment was beginning to feel the effects of the climate, and officers and men were going sick daily. Some shook off the malaria after a few days, but many others got so bad and had such repeated attacks that they had to be sent to the hospital ship at Delagoa, or else down country, many being eventually invalided home.

The three companies at Kaapmuiden left that station on the 14th January and arrived at Barberton the next morning. The night was passed at Avoca, as it was too dark to cross the river by the gimcrack arrangements in use there. These consisted of a dilapidated sort of raft which was worked on pulleys, and took about twenty men across in one journey, and a mid-air performance by which four men were swung over in a sort of basket from bank to bank. With the baggage, it took the four companies two hours to get across.

A short time before the train had run across at this point, but the temporary bridge had been swept away by a flood. The main bridge, higher up the river, had been destroyed by the Boers in the usual manner.

The remainder of the battalion arrived on the 16th and 17th, and we then, such of us as were left, found ourselves together again for the first time since September. The regiment was simply a wreck of its former self, and no less than ten officers and 300 men were in hospital. The majority of these went sick at Komati Poort, and many held out there till their arrival at Barberton, the change to a colder temperature evidently bringing out the fever.

During the first week of our arrival there were numerous alarms as to the near presence of a commando, and the usual reinforcing of the posts had to take place. The outpost duty was very hard, and being so short of officers and men, a company of the Royal Warwickshire had to be sent to help in the duties, and even with this addition, we were all, officers and men, four days off and four days on picquet, and, in addition, the men had various guards and duties to perform.

Barberton is a small mining town, containing about 4,000 inhabitants. It is picturesquely situated on the slope of some lofty hills, which seem to form a huge amphitheatre, the town being at the southern end. It is about 3,000 feet above the sea level.

The first mining camp of any importance in the Kaap valley was formed on some farms belonging to a Mr. Moodie, six miles west of Barberton, where, in December, the Boers captured the small mounted infantry picquet before alluded to. Exploitations for gold still further afield took place, and Moodie's sank into insignificance when the wealth of the famous Sheba Mountain was ascertained. Midway between Sheba and Moodie's camp, the town of Barberton sprang up in a single night, and became for a time the most important centre in the Transvaal.

The first regiment quartered here occupied the local club for their mess, which we in turn took over from the Royal Scots. It was a comfortable place, with billiard-room, mess and anterooms, and there were small quarters for the officers, overlooking the garden. The men were accommodated all over the town in the various shops and houses, which had been vacated by their owners. There was a good market every Saturday morning, and we were able to get pineapples, mangoes, bananas and grapes, besides fresh eggs and vegetables at a very moderate price. The pines were very plentiful and good, and were sometimes issued as a ration to the troops by the O/C Supplies.

When at Barberton we were allowed to get up a considerable amount of baggage which had accumulated at Bloemfontein. Our drums also were sent up from the Cape, but we had some difficulty in getting enough men to form a respectable band.

On the 23rd of January we heard of the lamented death of Her Majesty Queen Victoria, and on the Sunday following our chaplain, the Rev. R. Armitage, held a solemn memorial service.

To help us in our picquet work, the men were encouraged to train dogs in outpost duty. As the dogs impressed for this service were not of a very intelligent breed, their efforts met with but poor success, the animals failing to realise the extreme importance of sentry duty. Once, when an officer was visiting his posts in the early morning, to see that his men were standing to arms, he heard a loud snoring on approaching the group. Concluding that one of the men was still asleep, he asked the corporal in charge for an explanation. "Oh, I beg pardon, Sir," said he, " that's only the outpost dog!"

The hills on which we had picquets were called respectively South, East, Abbot's and Scots'. The last named was easy of access, but the men carrying their blankets and great-coats found it hard work getting to the top of the others, and it took them over an hour to accomplish the ascent Water, fuel, and rations were carried up to these posts by mules. Once on the top, a splendid view to the north could be had for many miles, but the southern side was effectively blocked by the hills which rose still higher in front of the sentries.

There must have been many miles of good barbed wire used in the defences of Barberton, and there ought to have been cheap fencing for the farmers when the war was over. We used to adorn the wire in many places with jam-pot tins, so that should anyone stumble against the fencing, the jam-pot would give the alarm. This, however, was not without its disadvantages, as on a windy night the jam-pots often became very unruly. Then we had mines, too, laid about all over the place, and we longed to see one of them fired.

We remained together at Barberton till the 10th of April, when we were ordered to relieve the Royal Warwickshire detachments at Avoca and Kaapmuiden. Accordingly on that date, Lieutenant Walker and twenty men proceeded to the former, and A and C, consisting of only seventy men, departed for the latter station.

Kaapmuiden had greatly changed in its appearance since last we occupied it Commodious huts had been built on the old site of our camp, much more scrub had been cleared, and a very strong barbed wire entanglement surrounded the encampment Two strong blockhouses had been put up, and two more were in course of erection near the Kaap bridge, which had been reconstructed by the Royal Engineers, and the deviation was a thing of the past.

OFFICER'S SHELTER, SOUTH HILL, BARBERTON

ARRIVAL OF RATIONS ON SOUTH HILL, BARBERTON

Towards the end of April the 18th Brigade showed further signs of dissolution, for the departure of the Essex in October was followed by that of the Royal Warwickshire, who sailed shortly afterwards for the Bermudas. They had been more than decimated by their stay in the valley, and had hardly a man left for duty. Ceylon and St Helena were also rumoured as likely tonics for us, but somehow we managed to hang on, and avoided this prescription. The 2nd Battalion Hampshire Regiment relieved the Warwickshire, and at the same time released any detachments we had, except that of Avoca, whose garrison, consisting of an officer and twenty men, was changed every fortnight.

Whilst at Barberton we amused ourselves, when not on outpost, by cricket and football matches, tennis and shooting. The local club had two very good courts, and General Stephenson also had one at his quarters, where we often used to play.

Several of us also were granted leave to go and see the famous Sheba gold mine, twelve miles distant You could either ride there, or else going by train to Avoca, finish the journey on the little tramway line up to the mine. Mr. Russell, a well-known inhabitant of Barberton, was always kind enough to guide us there and explain the working of the mine to us.

On the 5th June a draft of 113 men arrived, under 2nd-Lieutenant Massy. 2nd-Lieutenants Marsden, McCall, Leatham and Nash-Wortham also joined us when at this station.

After being quartered for six months at Barberton, the battalion was once more transferred to Komati Poort and Kaapmuiden, arriving at these stations between the 9th and 12th July.

Lord Kitchener had taken over the command of the field force at the end of November, and was now perfecting his system of blockhouses on the railways and across country with the object of guarding the communications, and restricting the Boers in their movements over the *veldt*. We had to construct a few of these blockhouses at Barberton, and on taking over charge of the Delagoa line between Kaapmuiden and Komati, we found that we had to occupy thirty-eight blockhouses, extending from the Kaap bridge to the Komati River.

A, B, C, D and H companies, under Captain Orr, had their headquarters at Kaapmuiden, the remainder going as before to the Lebombo heights. These blockhouses were each occupied by a non-commissioned officer and four men, so that altogether 190 men were required for this duty, their relief taking place once a week. Rations and water were taken to them by special trains once in every two or three days.

The blockhouses in the Transvaal were made of any material handy, such as wooden sleepers, railway irons, stone and corrugated iron, and had the earth rammed between the walls, in order to make them bullet-proof. All those on the Kaapmuiden-Komati line were of this latter pattern, each being surrounded with a barbed wire entanglement, to prevent it being rushed, and were in every way impregnable except against artillery fire, but as the Boers were without guns towards the close of the war, this did not count for anything.

We found Lieutenant Matthews and thirty men of the 1st Volunteer Battalion already at Kaapmuiden, they having arrived a few days previously.

On the 22nd of July, 400 Boers attacked and captured Bremersdorp, which was held by forty of Steinacker's Horse. The latter, after some fighting, were forced to retire on Komati, after losing two maxims and several men killed and wounded.

This naturally created some excitement at Komati, as it was reported that the enemy were advancing in that direction. Fifty men were, therefore, ordered as reinforcements from Barberton, and fifty more were taken from Kaapmuiden, under Lieutenant Leatham. Parties under Captain Maitland, 2nd-Lieutenants Marsden and Nash-Wortham, were ordered into Swaziland to cover important points on the Boers' probable line of advance. These posts were, however, all withdrawn after a few days, as the Boers went off in another direction, having taken all the ammunition and stores they could lay their hands on in Bremersdorp.

Before leaving the Crocodile valley we had a few changes amongst the officers, Major Cotesworth having been detailed as president of a compensation board for damages incurred to property during the war, a duty which kept him away from the battalion for the rest of his time in South Africa. Captains Somervell and Lea joined at the end of July, the former from the Cape and the latter from home.

The Welsh Regiment had proceeded to Johannesburg in June, and the time had come for us, the last remaining battalion of the old 18th Brigade, to take our departure. We had been informed that it was not at all probable or desirable that we should spend another hot season in the Crocodile valley, and that September would likely see us on the move again, so we were not at all surprised when a wire came to Kaapmuiden, ordering the half-battalion there to start for Pretoria on the 11th August Accordingly, after being relieved by 300 men of the 2nd Battalion Duke of Cornwall's Light Infantry, A, B, C and H com-

SIGNALLING ON EAST HILL, BARBERTON

DEPUTATION FROM THE SWAZI QUEEN TO LORD KITCHENER,
SOUTH HILL, BARBERTON

panies, consisting of only 170 men and six officers, left on this date, and arrived at Pretoria at 12 (midnight) on the 12th, being joined by the headquarters and remaining companies a week later.

Nearly a year before the Green Howards had entered the Crocodile valley at Waterval-onder, and were then as fine a body of men as one could wish to see; perfect in health, and physically fit to go anywhere or perform any service.

What now remained of them passed through Onder on their return journey, every man saturated with malaria, and quite unable to do any really severe work, if called upon. To which may be attributed the fact, that we were kept on blockhouse duty on the railway during the remainder of the war, and took no part in convoy work or marching worth mentioning.

CHAPTER 7

Pretoria, Ladysmith, and the Rand

The four companies which arrived at Pretoria on the 12th August, marched the next morning to a camping ground near Arcadia bridge, within easy access of the town, where they got under canvas. The remainder of the regiment joined within a week, and we then relieved the 2nd Battalion 5th Fusiliers, taking over from them the eastern defences of the town. The volunteer detachment occupied the blockhouses at Koodoespoort, F company, East Fort, and A held the line as far as the Irene road. Headquarters were at Johnson's Redoubt, and G company was detailed as a guard over the Boer prisoners. There was also a small party of twenty men at Silverton.

B company, under Captain Somervell, marched out to Commando Nek, in the Magaliesburg range, about thirty miles distant

Coming up from the warmer climate of the valley, we thought we should have felt the change more, but the first ten days were hot enough for anyone camped in bell-tents, as we were. It, however, became much colder towards the end of August, and one day a terrific hailstorm burst over the whole camp. Few of us had ever seen anything like it It lasted for nearly half-an-hour, the hailstones being about the size of large marbles, and the noise they made beating on the canvas was deafening.

Pretoria certainly was wearing a more peaceful aspect than when we last saw it. Nearly all the shops were open, and we met in the streets more civilians and fewer soldiers. We got a morning paper from Natal, three days after publication, and we felt more in touch with home than we had been since we left Cape Town in December, 1899.

Our stay in the Transvaal capital was limited to three weeks only, for when Louis Botha with his commandoes threatened the Natal border in the middle of September, the Green Howards were amongst the troops that were hurried down to guard the colony.

We left on the 18th September, being confidentially informed that Ladysmith was our destination, and were relieved by the 1st Battalion Inniskilling Fusiliers.

It had been given out that we were bound for Kroonstad, there to relieve our 3rd Battalion but when we woke up the next morning we did not quite recognise the country. On arrival at Greylingstad, we were one and all convinced that Kroonstad had only been a blind, and that "the Garden Colony" was much more likely to be our address in future.

We spent two nights in the train, the men, as usual, being in open trucks. The rain simply came down in torrents each night of the journey, and they had, in consequence, a miserable time of it. It was nearly dark when we passed Majuba. There was a dense mist covering everything at the time, and we did not get even a glimpse of the historic hill.

None of the stations on this line looked particularly inviting, and reminded us very much of such places as Wonderfontein and Pan, on the Delagoa line, where so far we had escaped being quartered.

At Platrand we came across many old friends, as the Essex were there, still on their way to India.

We arrived at Ladysmith on the 20th, and marched through tons of mud up to "Tin Town," about two miles from the station. Tin Town really represents the ordinary barracks, which are generally occupied by the garrison quartered at Ladysmith in times of peace.

Two days after our arrival half the battalion was ordered to take up a line of outposts north of the town. *Sangar* building had now to be started afresh, for the old defences were in a very dilapidated condition. The remainder of the regiment was scattered about the railway line and district. We had posts as far as Colenso on the Durban line, and to Bester's on that of the Orange Colony. Added to this, 100 men, under Captain Esson, with Lieutenants Broun, Morgan and Matthews, proceeded to Van Reenen's Pass on the 7th October to act as a covering party during the erection of some blockhouses in the Drakensberg.

So far, from what we had seen, the scenery of the two Dutch republics had little in it to impress one very much. After the dreariness of the high *veldt*, the picturesque winding of the Crocodile River through the hills between Elandshoek and Kaapmuiden, rather ap-

East Hill, Pretoria

Shelters at Convent Hill, Ladysmith

peals to the traveller, as does the beautiful scenery round Barberton and the Kaap valley; but when he reaches the Drakensberg, he comes upon something quite out of the common, at any rate, in South Africa. The railway goes right up to the pass by a zigzag line, and as the train toils slowly along, the eye is at once struck by the strange shape of the fantastic peaks which tower above.

Pinnacles and huge masses of rock, bare of vegetation, rise up here and there in abrupt isolation on the mountain top, in striking contrast to the beautiful green *veldt* lying thousands of feet below, hemming in gorges so narrow, that as you peer down into them they scarcely seem wide enough to receive even the tiny rivulets which hurry through to join the streams of Natal.

There is a little hotel near Van Reenen's station, which gives accommodation to any chance visitors going to or returning from the Orange River Colony, as all trains remain there for an hour before resuming their journey to Harrismith or Ladysmith.

Part of the barracks at Tin Town were used as temporary quarters for the Boer prisoners, who kept arriving in batches from the north and west. When a large enough party had accumulated, it was our duty to escort it down country before it embarked for India, Ceylon, or St. Helena.

There were two sorts of prisoners, *tame* and *wild* ones. The former were *burghers* who had surrendered, and were given a certain amount of latitude, being permitted to go and come as they pleased all day long; but the latter, who were captured under arms and had refused to give in, were very strictly guarded. They spent a good deal of time playing cricket and tennis, and had an easy but monotonous time of it

Whilst at Ladysmith we were able to make excursions to Bulwana, Intombi, Wagon Hill, Caesar's Camp, etc., and were much interested, having heard so much about these places at the beginning of the war.

As our services were no longer required in Natal, consequent on the defeat of the Boers at Itala and Prospect, we left Ladysmith on the 21st October, and arrived at Elandsfontein on the morning of the 23rd, when we detrained, amidst pouring rain, and took over the outposts from the King's Own Yorkshire Light Infantry. Two days later we sent detachments of 100 men, under Captain Somervell, to Boksburg, and of sixty men to Springs; Boksburg is only six miles from Elandsfontein, and Springs, the terminus of the little branch line, twelve miles further on.

We occupied blockhouses north and east of Elandsfontein, and all the way along the line, both Boksburg and Springs having their own defences to be looked after as well.

On one of the last days of October, Colonel Benson's disastrous fight had taken place at Brakenlaagte, and a huge convoy arrived at Springs on the 4th November, bringing in the wounded, escorted by the 3rd 60th Rifles. Two wounded officers died on the way in, Lieutenant Maclean, of the Royal Artillery, and Lieutenant Martin, of the Yorkshire Light Infantry. We buried the latter at Elandsfontein, supplying the band and funeral party, whilst Lieutenant Maclean was buried at Springs by the 60th.

The Boers were very active in the neighbourhood of Springs at this time, and were constantly trying to surprise the column, which had its base there. We had to keep a very sharp lookout, and were assisted in this by having over twenty mounted men, chiefly belonging to A company. Patrols were sent out in a radius of seven miles round the station to look for the enemy, to watch the cattle, and prevent the natives from letting them stray too far.

In January we became more split up than ever, and a detachment of 100 men, under Captain Orr and Lieutenant Wardle, went to Vereeniging at the beginning of the month, so that we were pretty well divided between Elandsfontein, Boksburg, Springs, and Vereeniging.

During the summer the South African Constabulary had been pushing out a series of posts between the Delagoa and Natal railway lines, and had by this time advanced as far as the Wilge River, clearing the country on their way. The Boers, however, who numbered about 600, were constantly breaking back through these posts, and making themselves very troublesome. General G. Hamilton's column ran up against them near Nigel in December, when the Scots Greys had three officers killed and other casualties. Shortly afterwards they attacked the 28th M.I. near Klip *drift* in February, who suffered somewhat severely on this occasion.

On the 4th of February, about forty of them attacked Brakpan, six miles from Springs, but were driven off, and we picked up one dead and one badly wounded Boer in the morning.

On the 1st of April, Colonel Lawley's column fought an action at Boschman's Kop, eighteen miles south-east of Springs, neither side getting much advantage, the column losing two officers and ten men killed, and about sixty wounded.

Lord Kitchener's drives were now, however, beginning to tell on

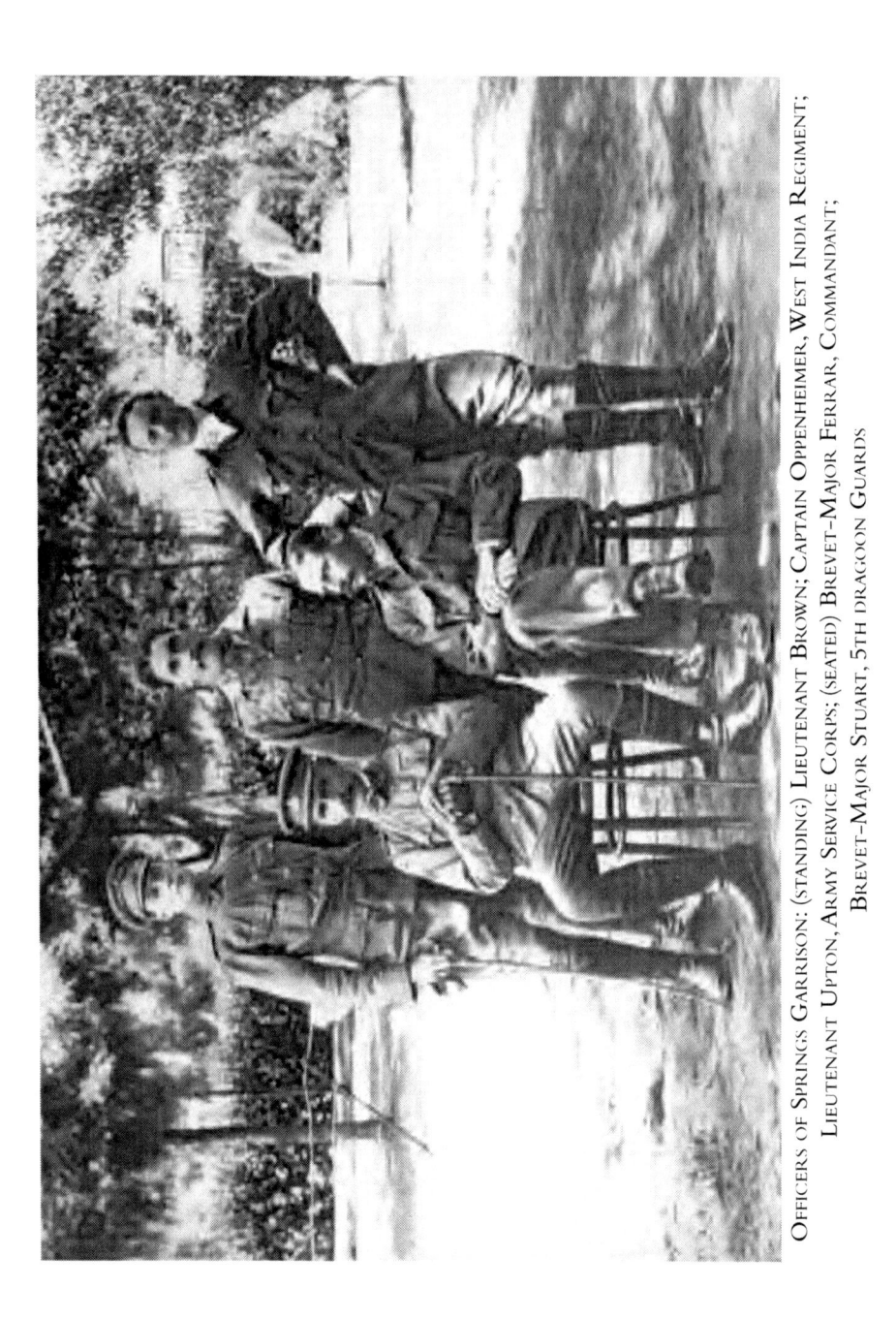

Officers of Springs Garrison: (standing) Lieutenant Brown; Captain Oppenheimer, West India Regiment; Lieutenant Upton, Army Service Corps; (seated) Brevet-Major Ferrar, Commandant; Brevet-Major Stuart, 5th dragoon Guards

the Boers, and in addition to the prisoners captured by the various columns, there were numerous surrenders, partly due to the approach of winter, as well as the want of proper food and clothing.

The battalion had little experience in these so-called *drives*, beyond holding the Springs-Elandsfontein line whilst columns were scouring the district. The Boers never attempted to cross the line, preferring the simpler plan of passing east of Springs, where there were never enough troops to stop them.

The drive that took place towards the end of April was hardly a success, as very few prisoners were taken, and most of the Boers broke through the Natal line, near Heidelberg. In connection with this drive, 500 men, consisting of Scots Guards, Gordon Highlanders and National Scouts, reinforced the Springs garrison, and formed a defensive line in a southerly direction. Thirteen columns were altogether employed, and in taking out a message to one of them, Private Wardle, of A company, was severely wounded and his horse shot.

Up to the end of June the battalion was split up between Springs, Boksburg, Elandsfontein, Vereeniging, Viljoen's *drift*, and Klip River station, A and C companies at Springs being more or less permanent, whilst the others were constantly changing.

The men felt the monotony of the blockhouse work very much. A sharp lookout for the enemy was always necessary, the posts had to be kept rationed with water and food daily, the defences were being continually improved, and trenches dug along the line. Signalling had to be kept up, and those who were mounted were well employed patrolling. So the days passed, and though there was lots of work, it was irksome in its regularity. Papers were a great boon, and literature of any kind was much appreciated.

A great relief to some was given by the transfer of 150 men to India, in exchange for a similar number, who arrived on the 3rd March at Elandsfontein, in charge of Captain Napier.

The question of peace now became the general subject of conversation, and everything pointed to a speedy termination of the war. Large batches of prisoners continued to be taken, many of them surrendering without making any fight, simply to "save their face." Those who had been coming in voluntarily to the line during the months of March and April had been in a woeful condition as regards their clothing. Some had no boots, others trousers made out of blankets and coats out of skins. The *veldt* was getting dried up, and there was nothing left for the horses to feed on.

We were not, therefore, surprised to hear that a meeting was to take place between the Transvaal and Free State leaders, and that a Conference was to be held at Vereeniging in the middle of May to discuss the question of terms of surrender.

Though our columns still kept the field, there was little fighting in this last fortnight of May. Rumours of peace grew apace, and at last, on May 31st, it became a reality, and the conditions of surrender were signed late that night at Pretoria.

When the public announcement was made on the 1st of June, we were naturally much relieved and delighted, but there was less excitement than might have been expected. Probably the long-deferred hope of it had made the fact difficult to realise.

A public thanksgiving service was held in Church Square, Pretoria, on Sunday, the 8th of June. Most of the regiments in the Transvaal and in the north of the Orange River Colony furnished detachments on this occasion at Pretoria, consisting each of one officer and forty non-commissioned officers and men, our representatives being drawn as far as possible equally from each company, all under command of Captain Esson. The regimental band accompanied the party. The aggregate of the detachments made up a total of 5,500 officers and men on parade, and the bands and various church choirs of Pretoria and Johannesburg churches provided the music. A platform had been erected in front of the Government buildings for the choirs and clergy, who belonged to every religious denomination in the colony.

At 1 p.m. punctually, Lord Kitchener appeared on the scene, and was received with a general salute.

After the service a verse of the national anthem was sung by all the soldiers and civilians with extraordinary enthusiasm, and the parade terminated with three cheers for His Majesty, called for by Lord Kitchener. These were given with a heartiness that can seldom ever have been equalled.

The campaign being now over, there is little more to be told. Our first batch of reservists, 100 strong, left on the 3rd of July, under Brevet-Major Holmes, being followed by 150, under Captain Esson and Lieutenant Broun, on 4th August, and a final party of forty-four, under Lieutenant Bastow, followed a fortnight later.

The health of the battalion had been very good during its stay at Elandsfontein and outlying stations.

From the 23rd October 1901, to August, 1902, out of an aver-

THE HORNETS' NEST, BLOCKHOUSE NEAR SPTINGS

age strength of 600, there had only been an average of twenty-four men in hospital. The number of admissions was 176, and there was only one death.

On the 4th September, the joyful news came that the Green Howards were to entrain that night for Cape Town. After a most comfortable journey, they arrived there on the 8th, and sailed in the *Lake Michigan* on the 12th, in company with the 3rd Battalion Grenadier Guards and the 1st Battalion Duke of Wellington's West Riding Regiment. After a smooth passage, the transport arrived at Southampton on the 13th of October, the regiment reaching Sheffield the same evening, having been absent from England two years and 325 days.

CHAPTER 8

The 2nd Battalion Mounted Infantry

Motto: *Nunquam dormio*

BREVETT-MAJOR M. H. TOMLIN'S NARRATIVE

On the outbreak of the Boer War, it will be remembered that the reinforcements first sent to South Africa consisted of some 50,000 men, including two cavalry brigades. With each of these cavalry brigades was sent a battalion of mounted infantry, drawn from the infantry battalions serving at home. Each battalion of M.I., to give them the name by which the force is now known, consisted of four companies, each of four sections, and two machine gun sections, so that men from eighteen different infantry battalions were serving in each regiment of M.I. It may be thought that this would entail a certain want of cohesion, but such was not the case. All the sections had been trained at home on the same system, and they soon merged their own identity into that of the 1st or 2nd M.I., as the two battalions were numbered. They were the original mounted infantry of the war, with the exception of the M.I. companies which were in South Africa, serving with their infantry battalions.

It is not proposed to discuss here the respective merits of the M.I. battalions formed by complete companies, or on the system above shown; it can be said, however, that those of us who were lucky enough to serve with the 2nd M.I., consider that the record of that battalion is one to be proud of.

The Green Howards' section was detailed as No. 3 section of the Northern company, 2nd Battalion M.I. This battalion formed part of the 2nd Cavalry Brigade, which was the old Union Brigade, famous for its exploits at Waterloo and Balaclava, but as a matter of fact, it never served as a brigade in South Africa, as the Royals went round to

Natal, whilst the Greys and Inniskillings formed part of Lord Roberts' army. Nor did the 2nd M.I. ever serve with a cavalry brigade as its M.I. force, on the principle worked out with such care. But *ex Africa semper aliquid novi* is as true now as when that much quoted remark was first made, and we all, horse, foot and artillery, changed a good many of our ideas as to how to make war before the 31st May, 1902.

To return to our section, which is at Aldershot mobilising. It consisted of one officer and thirty-five non-commissioned officers and men, of whom a list is given in the appendix.

The 2nd M.I. embarked in two parties, half a battalion in each, the Northern and Western companies, with headquarters, sailing from Tilbury on October 22nd in the *Orient*. The 73rd Highlanders were also on board. Fog delayed our start for two days, and we arrived at St.Vincent on November 1st, where we heard the news about Nicholson's Nek.

A considerable number of hardened pessimists had been very gloomy till then, as the telegram about Elandslaagte, which we had seen before sailing, had convinced them that war would be over before we reached the Cape. However, the news they heard at St Vincent made them come to the conclusion that there would probably be some fighting after we arrived, and that they would not miss the opportunity of gaining honours and fame.

We arrived at Cape Town on November 14th, after a most comfortable voyage, and entrained for De Aar on the 15th, where we arrived two days later. De Aar is a very dusty place, and the companies were not sorry to move on the 18th to Naaupoort, whence they moved to join General French's force in the Colesberg district We had brought our saddlery with us from England, and we were given ponies from the remount establishment at De Aar during our day's stay there. They were a particularly good lot of country-bred ponies, and they stood the hard work to which they were subjected very well. Two only finished the campaign to my knowledge, ridden by Lieutenant Heath and Colour-Sergeant Stretch respectively; at least, these were the only two still with the 2nd M.I., though I daresay there were others, which having been left behind at veterinary hospitals, were reissued to other corps. I must not forget old Marchioness, an Irish pony brought out by Captain Brooke, of the King's Own Yorkshire L.I., who commanded the western company at the beginning, and the battalion at the end of the war. Marchioness, after several attacks of *trekkitis*, which reduced her to a skeleton, at the end of the war was fat and well, and quite ready to start on three years' more campaigning.

Abler and more virulent pens have dealt with the remount question, nor has there been any lack of abuse showered on the equipment given to the army. I know of one set of saddlery which I (as acting quartermaster) issued to my groom, Private Hodge, at De Aar in November, 1899, and which lasted him till 31st August, 1902, on which day he handed it into store at Bloemfontein before going home. As he had not missed one day of the campaign, and as the 2nd M.I. made a rule of never halting more than the inside of a week at any particular place, it will be admitted that that set of saddlery, at all events, was a good one. The general experience was that all articles from Government factories were good, and, if taken care of, lasted as well as could be desired. The enormous waste came from the idle carelessness of some of the individuals serving in the army.

During the last tour of home service of the 1st Battalion Green Howards, only one section of M.I. had been trained. This was at the Curragh in 1897, under Lieutenant Walker. Of this section there were not many left in the battalion at the end of 1899, and, consequently, the section was completed with men who had been trained with the 2nd Battalion in India and had come home again. None of them were reservists.

On January 18th, 1900, I left the 2nd M.I., on being appointed to the headquarter staff, and from that day to May 31st, 1901 (when Lieutenant Walker joined), the section was without an officer of the regiment. The responsibility devolved on the capable shoulders of Sergeant Wilson, who acquitted himself well of the task.

M. H. Tomlin

Account Compiled by Private Sidney Fallowell from His Diary

On the 7th February, the 2nd M.I. left the Colesberg district by train for the Orange River. We crossed it on the 9th, and arrived two days later at Ramdam, getting to the Modder River on the 15th, with the 6th Division close behind us. We bivouacked on the south side, and moved off next morning at 3 a-m., taking with us rations of compressed beef for four days. We were engaged with the Boers at the battle of Klip *drift*, and crossed the river several times during the day. We met the 4th M.I., who were also having a warm time of it. We, unfortunately, lost most of our rations, as owing to the galloping, the straps round the tins became loose, and the latter fell off. Captain Hart, commanding our company, was wounded, Lieutenant Courtenay, of the Dublin company, was killed, and we had several other casualties.

We had all been along the river bank in small parties, but assembled together in the evening as far as was practicable, and bivouacked on the south side.

On the 17th we crossed the Modder at dawn, and in our advance passed many dead horses. A woman at a farm told us that Cronje had asked her to go with him, but that she had refused. She showed good sense. We made slow progress, and at 4.30 p.m., halted, being relieved by the 6th M.I. Crossed once more to the south side, no one troubling much about food or anything else, as we were all dead beat. On again next morning, the bill of fare, owing to loss of rations, being very simple; hard biscuit and water for breakfast, same for dinner, and, if any biscuit was left, we enjoyed the same for tea; if not, we did without it. We did not take a very active part in this first day's fighting at Paardeberg, as we were escort to some guns, from which position we had a good view of the battle. Up to the time Cronje surrendered we were constantly reconnoitring and fighting, and as there was a lot of rain, we had a hard time of it. After the surrender we moved off east, about seven miles, to a good camping ground, where there was water, firewood, and grass for our ponies quite close to us. The latter fared better than we did, for we had only a handful of flour each day with no baking powder.

On the advance being resumed on the 7th March, we very soon came under fire from the Boer position. We drove them out, but we could not help ourselves to the good things they left behind in their hurry, simply because our captain would not let us.

On the 10th, we were on right flank guard, and had not gone far when one of us asked a *kaffir* if he had seen any Boers. The boy pointed to some hills about four miles away, and said they were full. Lieutenant Geary now sent over a message, saying he wanted reinforcements. He had been moving on our left. The Green Howards' section was sent to help him. We were soon in action, and on my way to the top of a *kopje* I passed the dead body of Private Hudson, Hampshire section. This was the commencement of the battle of Driefontein. During the engagement A company of my regiment passed close to me, and I noticed Private Hughes badly wounded. We had a lot of fighting all day, but there were very few casualties in the 2nd M.I. We went on picquet duty at dusk, and two hours later were relieved by the Grenadier Guards.

On the morning of the 14th we marched into Bloemfontein, a day after the official entry.

Leaving a fever-stricken city behind us, I and a few others took some sick horses out to Fischer's farm, about seven miles west of Bloemfontein. Most of us were rather run down in health, chiefly caused by insufficient food and bad water, combined with very hard work.

I rejoined the 2nd M.I. at Karee on the 7th April. Our camp there was prettily situated, the only complaint being that the water was a long way off. We had a lot of rain, and many men fell sick. On the 13th, we were relieved by the 4th M.I., amongst whom I saw a good number of my regimental comrades. The next day, in company with the Royal Sussex Regiment, we made a reconnaissance, coming in range of the enemy, who were in some *kopjes* north of our camp, and who soon let us know it. The infantry replied with volleys, and the pom-pom rattled off two belts of its awful shells. We then retired to camp, had breakfast, and then marching *via* Glen, reached the outskirts of Bloemfontein on the 20th April.

We were only a few hours in this camp, when we were ordered to go out to Thaba N'chu. Here we had two severe days' fighting, and Private Humphries, of my section, was killed. So was Lieutenant Geary, of our company.

Under Major-General Ian Hamilton, our force, consisting of the cavalry under Colonel Broadwood, the M.I. under Colonel Ridley, and the infantry brigades of Brigadier-Generals Smith Dorrien and Bruce Hamilton, began its advance on Pretoria.

We came in for sniping every day until we reached Winburg on the 5th April. So as to be near good water, we moved about five miles further north, and rested for three days.

We had no more severe fighting till we reached the Zand River, where the Boers held a formidable position. In the afternoon they set fire to the *veldt*, and retired under cover of the smoke.

Our next important day was the entering of Kroonstad, where we arrived a few hours after Lord Roberts. Thence we went eastwards to Lindley, and then on to Heilbron, fighting rearguard actions all the way.

The Queen's birthday was ushered in by a salute from the *burghers*. We were in the rearguard again, and our guns had to be requisitioned to keep them back. In the evening we joined on to the 11th Division. Songs were sung ail day over the large camping ground.

When we resumed our march we moved over to the left of the

main line of railway, for up to this time we had been on the right. On the 26th of May we crossed the Vaal at Boschbank *drift*. Our rations were running short, and three biscuits were issued to each man, who was told that he might not get any more for some time. On reaching Dornkop, we were ordered to canter up to take part in what everyone thought was going to be a great battle. It lasted all day, and left us with many casualties. Under cover of night, the Boers retired.

We bivouacked at Florida, a few miles further on, where we gathered a good supply of *mealies* for our horses. By the 2nd June we were so hard up for food that we were allowed to eat our emergency rations. On the 4th, when nearing Pretoria, we were told that the town had surrendered, but as we were under fire at the time, we thought that there must be some mistake. It was, however, true, and on the 5th we marched through Pretoria, and bivouacked at Silverton. The next day we went to a pretty place called Irene. Returning to Pretoria on the 9th, we learned that hostilities were suspended for forty-eight hours, and the rumour gained ground that the Boers were going to surrender, but as nothing more was heard, we concluded we should have to fight.

On the 11th June the battle of Diamond Hill commenced. We had a very heavy day's fighting, and many casualties in our division, which was engaged on the left of the Boer position. On the 14th, the enemy were driven out, and we followed them up a short way, crossing the railway at Elands River. Then we returned to Pretoria, and bivouacked at Sunnyside. Here we stayed for a few days, and then departed south with three days' rations of *mealie* meal. Marching by Heidelberg, we entered Frankfort on the 1st July, the Boers retiring before us. By this time we expected to meet the Highland Brigade with supplies, but were disappointed. The next day, 300 men, composed of 200 M.I. and 16th Lancers, were sent out under Colonel Little to look for the absent brigade, and after *trekking* for about nine miles, we heard the pipers playing. We then halted, and the advance guard of the brigade, when they saw us, at once opened fire, and wounded three horses before they discovered their mistake. We then escorted them into camp. Marching by Reitz, we bivouacked at Bethlehem on the 8th July.

A few days later I proceeded with a number of men from other corps to fetch remounts from Kroonstad. We halted on the 13th at Heilbron, and bivouacked near the spot where De Wet had captured one of our mail trains. Letters and newspapers covered the ground for a considerable distance.

On approaching Kroonstad, we were ordered to change our direction and go to Lindley. We could only proceed very slowly, for our cattle were in very poor condition, and many oxen were dying each day.

At dawn, on the 19th, we encountered the Boers, and at once got our wagons into as small a space as possible. Every man was now called upon to use his rifle, and we had a few hit in attacking a *kopje*, where we found three wounded Boers, one of them nearly dead. Fighting continued till dusk.

This party of the enemy was no doubt composed of those who, under De Wet, had escaped from the Wittebergen cordon, leaving Prinsloo behind to surrender. The O/C troops, Kroonstad, knowing we were coming in, sent out to meet us, and then we were hurried on towards Lindley, so as to hold De Wet back until Major-General Broadwood came up behind him. In this we miserably failed, for had De Wet had time to spare to fight us, he would no doubt have surrounded our small force, and compelled its surrender. As it was, he had to push on, knowing he was pursued by General Broadwood.

We rejoined the 2nd M.I. on the 26th July near Vredefort. There was a rumour that the Boers were surrounded. Troops were arriving all day, and it really looked as if it would be another Paardeberg. Trenches were made in front of camp, and everyone seemed confident of the Boers' surrender. But notwithstanding all our precautions, De Wet broke away north during the first week in August. One of these days, when out reconnoitring under Lieutenant Murdoch, we had a very warm time of it We had ridden up to a *kopje*, and on being ordered to halt the officer pulled out his field glasses, scanned the summit, and said he thought there were no Boers on it. Owing to the nature of the ground we had to advance in rather close formation, and were at once greeted with a heavy fire.

A man of the Royal Irish Fusiliers was taken prisoner, Lieutenant Murdoch's horse was hit, and Heeley, of my section, had his rifle knocked out of his hand; Davis got a bullet through his sleeve, and my horse was also wounded before we got out of range.

We had to follow the enemy up across the Vaal, over the Gatsrand and across the railway at Velvediend, pushing them so hard that they left their wagons burning on the road, and released Private Whelan, who had been taken prisoner on August 1st. With hardly any rest, we kept on their trail, only to hear that Oliphant's Nek, in the Magaliesberg, was not held and that De Wet, to our intense mortification, had passed through it.

Then came the news that Colonel Hore, with a small force, was surrounded on the Elands River, and we moved off to relieve him. This being accomplished, on the 15th August we then made for Rustenburg and Wolhuter's Kop. Here De Wet and his *burghers* were seen crossing the Magaliesberg, but though they were well within range, and we had a battery of R.H.A. with us, not a shot was fired; at the time they were taken for Roberts' Horse.

On the 24th we arrived at Pretoria, and had a long-wished-for rest, getting a new fit out from top to toe, our first since leaving England.

We went on *trek* again on the 4th September, and for the next three months were patrolling and constantly fighting in the Hekpoort and Magaliesberg districts, under Major-General Clements. I need scarcely dwell on our work now, for it was simply a matter of marching and losing men daily, it being a question whether we would catch the *burghers* napping or they would catch us. The infantry kept searching the hills, whilst we moved in the valleys. Some ghastly sights were met with, and a young soldier of the 5th Fusiliers one day came across four natives, not only shot, but with their throats cut also.

On the way into Krugersdorp, which we reached on the 12th November, we were sniped at all the way from every nook and dell, without having the advantage of getting a shot back in return. We stayed in the town for a day or two, and were then off again, soon to be busy scrapping again with Delarey.

On the 7th December we were camped at Nooigedacht. Our force at this time numbered scarcely 1,200 men, under command of Major-General Clements. It was made up of Kitchener's Horse, Imperial Yeomanry, 2nd M.I., one 4-7in., one pom-pom, four guns P Battery R.H.A., half and Battalion King's Own Yorkshire L.I., half 2nd Battalion 5th Fusiliers. Colonel Legge (20th Hussars) was in command of the mounted troops, Colonel Cookson being second in command.

All the troops, with the exception of the Imperial Yeomanry and K.O.Y.L.I., were bivouacked west of a small but fast-running stream, which flowed from a *nek* in the mountain to a river in the valley on the south side. The 5th Fusiliers had their bivouac on the summit of the Magaliesberg, and had to climb up the *nek* to get to it An under-feature, starting twenty feet below the top, slopes gradually towards the valley west of the stream. These twenty feet are very steep, and a ladder would be necessary to get from hill to mountain, so to speak.

The 2nd M.I. found the picquet for this hill. Early in the morning, about 3.30 a.m., shots were heard, and almost immediately heavy

CAPTAIN AND ADJUTANT R. P. L. VIGORS, 2ND M. I.

SERGEANT-MAJOR WORTHING, 2ND M. I.

firing commenced. The picquet was at once reinforced, and on Captain Atkins arriving with supports, he found the men retiring, but fighting for their ground against long odds. He soon pulled the men together, and, confident of success, the 2nd M.I. and Kitchener's Horse, who had also come up, slowly pushed the Boers backwards. The firing at this point was continuous, and at very short range, so close, in fact, that our men and the Boers were found nearly side by side. Though many of our officers fell at the beginning of the fight, we drove the Boers slowly down the hillside, which was covered with short trees. We made a few prisoners, but had the enemy been followed to the base, a larger number must have been caught, as that was where they left their horses.

The Boers now galloped westwards, being shelled by two 12-pounders and a pom-pom, which had been ordered up to the picquet hill. Our killed and wounded were being carried down to camp, and, with the exception of the guns, all firing had ceased. Everyone thought the attack was over, and General Clements told Colonel Cookson that we could go to breakfast, leaving Kitchener's Horse and the guns on the hill.

Before we got to the bottom of the slope, we noticed that the two guns left in camp were shelling the summit of the Magaliesberg, on which the Fusiliers were camped, and we could see that a fight was taking place, as the Boers were firing from the edge of the cliff. We never for a moment doubted but that the 5th would hold their own until reinforcements reached them, and which were being dispatched at the time from the K.O.Y.L.I. and Yeomanry.

The Boers had retired westwards from the picquet hill, and had reached the summit of the range by means of a *kloof*, so that once they gained the edge of the cliff, they flanked those on the top, and it was also an easy thing for them to pour lead into us down below. Before the reinforcements reached the Fusiliers, the latter had surrendered, leaving the Boers at liberty to shoot our men down as fast as they showed themselves.

In the meantime we returned to the picquet hill, but did not remain there long, being ordered to retire to some hills about 2,000 yards south-east of camp. The guns were ordered to fire and limber up in succession, pom-pom last, and Captain Brooke collected as many men as he could to cover their retirement. In the camp itself great difficulty was experienced in getting away the spare horses from the 2nd M.I. lines, owing to the heavy fire from the cliff. One of the guns of

P Battery had been moved up from camp to defend the *nek*, and almost every man had fallen. Chiefly through the exertions of Colour-Sergeant Smith, who, with twenty men, went to their assistance, the gun was brought under cover of an outhouse, where it was limbered up, but the party did not return so strong as it had started. An attempt was made to load a wagon with S.A.A., and two *kaffirs* were set on the move with it, but it did not go far before several of the mules were knocked over, and the ammunition lost.

When we reached the hills to which we had been ordered to retire, our guns again got into action. As the Boers now had an open plain to cross to get at us, they had no easy task, despite their numbers; in fact, they did not once try in earnest. The majority of them were soon feasting on the food we had been forced to leave behind us. About 3.30 p.m., we continued our retirement towards Pretoria, fighting rear and flank guard actions till dark. We continued marching during the night, arriving close to Commando Nek about 5 a.m. on the 14th December.

In this fight the 2nd M.I. lost heavily. Three officers, Captain Atkins (Wiltshire Regiment), Lieutenant Murdoch (Cameron Highlanders), and Lieutenant Reid (Somersetshire L.I.) were killed, in addition to fifteen men, whilst Captain Sandilands and Lieutenant the Hon. Clegg Hill were wounded, besides many men.

We succeeded in saving the guns and nearly all General Clements' wagons, but the 2nd M.I. and Kitchener's Horse lost everything. The attack on the picquet was, in my opinion, only a feint, while the main attack took place on the ridge occupied by the 5th Fusiliers. It was certainly a defeat for us, but it was not a disaster, as we saved our guns and nearly all the baggage and ammunition.

From Commando Nek we went on to Rietfontein, and arrived at Pretoria on the 19th, where we were again issued with new saddles, clothes, etc.

I remained here, having an attack of fever, and did not rejoin the 2nd M.I. till the 1st February, when I found them in the Gatsrand Mountains. During the month we were operating between the Vaal River and the Krugersdorp-Klerksdorp railway.

On the 7th March, as we were moving through the hills towards Krugersdorp, the Boers attacked our rearguard, their numbers increasing as time wore on. The road was heavy, and our convoy moved slower and slower, making things difficult for us, and what was worse, a mist was rising. We had an awkward pass to cross, and each wagon wanted two teams of mules before we could get it to move. As we neared the pass, the Boers pressed on, forcing the 8th M.I. to close on the convoy. Had it not been for Lieutenant Spring (Lincolnshire Regiment) rushing for a position with his own and the Green Howards' section, the Boers would probably have caused a stampede among the convoy animals waiting to cross the pass, whilst the *kaffirs* would have bolted. The situation can be more readily imagined than described. The enemy, however, were kept back, and we arrived safely at Krugersdorp late in the evening, wet through to the skin, for it had commenced to rain, and with our bivouac on the cold, wet ground, the most miserable day of the whole campaign came to an end.

We entrained for Potchefstroom on the 8th March, and operated in that district for the rest of the month.

On the 23rd we marched early, having General Babington's troops on our right, some few miles distant We came up with the Boers and had some fighting, but the day closed without incident The next day we were at it again by 5.30 a.m., and were pressing hard on the enemy. We galloped about ten miles (being accompanied by our ammunition and Cape carts only), and on crossing a *drift*, found seven deserted wagons. Then we met with a gun and two artillery men who had been captured by our advance guard, and finally came in sight of the whole of the Boer convoy. It consisted of forty bullock wagons, a large number of Cape carts, loose bullocks, etc, two guns, one pom-pom, five maxims, accompanied by 139 Boers. All were captured at 10 a.m., after a most exciting chase.

On the 13th April, Captain Tomlin rejoined the regiment, and took over command of the Northern company in time to share in a successful night march, which resulted in the recapture of a gun taken from O Battery R.H.A. at Nitral's Nek, a pom-pom, and, besides transport, about fifty prisoners.

The column was operating in the Klerksdorp-Ventersdorp district, General Babington being in supreme command. We were engaged nearly every day, and when the column was not moving, convoys had to be escorted to the railway, so that there was not much rest for the mounted troops.

During May we were *trekking* through the very difficult country to the east of the Mafeking line, and the horses suffered a good deal from bad water. The country was of a poor type; flat plains, covered with high grass, with many holes and ant-heaps; no trees, no water, and such farms as there were, were miserable places, very different from the country round Klerksdorp, where we arrived again at the end of May.

At this time the battalion was serving in Sir H. Rawlinson's column, with which it remained till the end of the war.

At Klerksdorp, Lieutenant Walker joined, and took over command of the Green Howards' section. Having filled our wagons, we *trekked* off on the 31st May, and a week later got in touch with the Boers south of Oliphant's Nek. We pitched our camp at Vlakfontein, the scene of Colonel Dixon's fight a few days before. Next morning we moved westwards, and on the 8th June got into action early, and captured fourteen Boers, twenty-seven wagons, in addition to sheep and oxen. On this occasion Captain Tomlin, in a most daring manner, rode with twenty men through a deep *kloof* to the head of the convoy and stopped it, under a heavy fire. For this service he was mentioned in despatches.

During the remainder of June and July we were working in the Zeerust district, frequently in connection with Lord Methuen, and our united efforts resulted in considerable damage to the local commandoes.

The country was very fine, well watered and wooded, very hilly, and a hundred men could have hid in any of the *kloofs* without being seen from the road. The farms had a well-to-do appearance, especially round Rustenberg, where the late president had taken the best of the land.

On the 24th July our old section leader, Sergeant Wilson, left us to rejoin the regiment at Pretoria. We were all very sorry to lose him, for he had always treated us well, and none of us ever want to serve under a better non-commissioned officer.

On the 25th we camped at Potchefstroom, and the next day moved off towards the Vaal, meeting Colonel Garratt's force on the 27th. The same afternoon we crossed the river at Lindeque *drift*, surprising a party of Boers, who were unable to evade us, and after a good ride, we succeeded in capturing fourteen prisoners and sixteen wagons. We marched on towards Bloemfontein, reaching Glen on the 11th August. having captured a few prisoners and large numbers of cattle on the way. We continued our course until we reached Wepener, and then made for Aliwal North, where we arrived on September 12th. Long marches, without the chance of a meal and little or no rest, was the order for each and every day. We were constantly engaged with the *burghers*, but they were not in large numbers, and were not over anxious to fight, so that the damage inflicted on them was never very great.

From Aliwal North we moved into Cape Colony, but at Burghersdorp orders were received for our brigade to entrain for the north, and we arrived at Elandsfontein on the 24th September, whence we marched to Heidelberg.

On the 5th October, we made a night march from Greylingstad, and just before dawn commenced to gallop after the enemy. We kept up a good pace for a few hours, only halting for a few minutes to roll our greatcoats. A good many of the men had to fall back, as their horses could not keep up, but Lieutenant Walker went on, with only a few of us following. The Boers now made a stand, and a retirement had to be made, in face of their superior numbers. A sergeant's horse of the Bedfordshire section was killed, and Lieutenant Walker returned under fire and helped him along to safety, for which act he was mentioned in despatches.

On the 7th, we had another night march, and on daylight appearing, gave chase again. The northern company followed the Boers up for many miles, losing one man killed and two wounded. We picked up one dead Boer.

During the month of November our column was working round Standerton, and on December 2nd arrived at Ermelo. Every house in the place was destroyed except one, which was occupied by a German lady. I don't know what became of her.

We were now working in conjunction with the columns under Major-General Bruce Hamilton, and a succession of night marches during December accounted for close on 400 Boers in killed, wounded, and prisoners.

On the 15th January, 1902, we left Ermelo for Standerton, and for the rest of the month operated in the Vrede district. Then we took part in the drives which had now been organised, our first ending at Wolverhoek on the 8th of February, and there was another soon after near Harrismith. I am sorry I cannot describe the doings of the 2nd M.I. at about this period, as I was absent, owing to an attack of enteric fever, from the 11th January till the 20th April, when I rejoined at Klerksdorp.

We moved out from the town on the 23rd, and on May 6th were camped at Klein Palmeitfontein, where we commenced the last drive which was to take place. We marched north-west, and suffered much inconvenience from a scarcity of water for both ourselves and horses.

On the 10th, we came up to the Boers and captured thirteen men and ten wagons. The latter were loaded with blankets, kits, etc., which had belonged to the Yeomanry of Lord Methuen's force. The end of our drive found us at Devondale siding, on the Mafeking railway. After a few days, we marched to Klerksdorp, arriving there on the 22nd May. Here we remained, waiting for the result of the Boers' conference amongst themselves as to whether it was worth while carrying on a struggle with everything against them. The end came at last, and on the 1st of June, after service, for it was a Sunday, Colonel Rawlinson read us out the following telegram:

Peace was signed last night.

I need scarcely add more, but before closing this somewhat incomplete record of the doings of the 2nd M.I., I should like to state that the battalion marched since February, 1900, not including any operation where the convoy was not taken, a total distance of 8,453 miles.

Sidney Fallowell

CHAPTER 9

The 4th Battalion Mounted Infantry

Previous to the departure of the Green Howards from England to the seat of war, orders were received for the formation of a company of mounted infantry on the arrival of the regiment in Cape Colony. Major G. C. S. Handcock was appointed to the command, with 2nd-Lieutenants W. G. Tarbet and M. H. Nevile as his subalterns.

A few days after the battalion had arrived at De Aar, the company, which was over 130 strong of all ranks, was issued with horses, saddlery, etc., and joined at De Aar the Cork company of the 1st M.I., under Colonel Alderson. The mounted company of the Warwickshire Regiment was formed at the same time, and was also attached to the 1st M.I.

On the 20th January, 1900, half the company was ordered to form part of a mixed mounted force under Colonel Alderson, with the object of marching on Prieska, in Griqualand West, and proceeding against the colonial rebels, who for some time past had been making raids on the town and district, and disturbing the loyalists.

The little force consisted altogether of half the Green Howards' company, half the Warwickshire company, the Cork company, a detachment of N.S. Wales Mounted Rifles, a section of the R.F.A., and two guns of the Cape Artillery.

At 2 p.m. on the 22nd, the column started from camp, Major Handcock and 2nd-Lieutenant Tarbet accompanying it, 2nd-Lieutenant Nevile being left behind with the other half company. The force marched fifteen miles in the afternoon, and bivouacked on the Shulefontein farm, on the Britstown road. Starting early the next day, they arrived at Britstown at noon. Owing to the excessive heat and rate of marching (trotting and walking alternately), many of the horses got knocked up, and during the rest of the expedition the main body was rarely allowed to move faster than a walk.

Haudwater was reached on the 24th, where the Warwickshire company was left as a help to the garrison. Twenty-five miles was accomplished the next day, the column halting and bivouacking at Omdrai Vlei, where there was a large ostrich farm, owned by an Englishman named Devenish, who showed great hospitality to the officers.

When the column moved on towards Prieska next morning, the Yorkshire half-company was ordered to remain behind to escort an ox convoy with supplies for the troops. This convoy started at sunset, and passing through a gap in a long range of *kopjes*, known as Doornberg Nek, outspanned for a few hours, purposing to resume the march at dawn. Karabee was reached the same day, where the convoy had hardly arrived, when Colonel Alderson sent back word that he was returning from Prieska. The reason for this was that all the mounted infantry were ordered to mass at Orange River station preparatory to Lord Roberts' invasion of the Free State. Colonel Alderson's commando was now considerably increased by the addition of the troops garrisoning Prieska, *viz.*, the Eastern company 2nd M.I., a company of N.S. Wales Mounted Rifles, some of Remington's Scouts, and a party of Roberts' Horse. The whole force reached Orange River station on the 2nd February, and encamped on the north bank.

Since leaving De Aar Junction on the 22nd January, the half company under Major Handcock and 2nd-Lieutenant Tarbet had been on the move nearly every day, and the men were rapidly getting into condition for the more serious work before them.

Colonel Alderson now left the station, taking with him the 1st M.I., and the Yorkshire company was detailed to form part of the 4th Battalion, one of the many which were fast being raised by drafts from all the infantry regiments in the field force. The greater part of the 4th M.I. were at De Aar, under command of Lieutenant-Colonel Henry, 5th Fusiliers, and on the 7th February they arrived at Orange River. The four regiments representing it were the Royal Warwickshire, the Princess of Wales's Own (Yorkshire), the Duke of Cornwall's L.I. and the King's Shropshire L.I.

On the 9th, the whole M.I. Division, numbering about eight battalions, under command of Colonel Hannay, Argyle and Sutherland Highlanders, crossed the Orange River bridge, and bivouacked about seven miles north. The next morning they entered the enemy's country at Ramah, a small farm where a halt was made, to wait for a large convoy which was being escorted to the army at Ramdam, where they arrived on the 12th February.

The 4th M.I. next day marched to Waterval *drift*, and resting there till nightfall, encamped next morning near a farm called Wegdrai, about four miles south-east of Jacobsdal, on the banks of the Riet River. Here the outposts, composed of Kitchener's Horse, were attacked by the Boers, and on being reinforced by the 4th M.I., the enemy retired, after half an hour's fighting. The battalion now advanced on Jacobsdal, the Yorkshire company working round the left flank. The latter did not again come under fire, but the Cornwall and Shropshire companies had a few men hit, whilst Colonel Henry was wounded and taken prisoner.

Major Handcock was now in command, and about midnight of the 14th started off with the battalion as escort to a convoy to Klip *drift*, which was reached at 7 a.m.

On the 15th February, late at night, orders were received to march at 4 a.m. in the morning in a northerly direction. The Modder was crossed about an hour before sunrise, and after a lapse of two or three hours, heavy firing was heard on the right, and it was found that Cronje's force, retiring from Majersfontein, had been met with. The fighting that morning fell to the 13th Brigade (General Knox's) of the 6th Division.

About 11 a.m. the 4th M.I. began to follow up the enemy to try and effect some damage before nightfall. The Green Howards' company had about three miles to gallop, and crossed the river twice before coming up with Cronje's rearguard. Fighting now took place, and eventually the battalion had to retire on Klip *drift*. 2nd-Lieutenant Tarbet and Private Hamley were both slightly wounded, and there were about thirteen men killed and wounded in the remainder of the battalion, besides many horses drowned in the Modder.

After this engagement the battalion was split up into two parties, one being under Captain Everitt, adjutant to Colonel Henry, and the other under Colonel Henry himself, who had returned, having been rescued by the 7th Division.

On the 17th this latter party, with Major Handcock, 2nd-Lieutenant Nevile, and part of the Yorkshire company, marched in the direction of Paardeberg, arriving there on the morning of the 18th, and were fighting unceasingly all day in various parts of the field.

On the 19th, the Yorkshire company were once more together, and were sent on outpost to a farm about six miles north of the *laager*, and up to the time that Cronje surrendered, were constantly engaged. They remained in much the same place on outpost duty till the 7th March, when the main body of the whole force marched straight on Poplar Grove.

The 4th and 6th M.I. were, however, ordered to make a demonstration on the left, the Green Howards performing the duties of advanced and left flank guard. After about two hours' march, a large open plain was reached, bounded on the east by a range of formidable-looking *kopjes*. The Shropshire and Cornwall companies found the Boers with a pom-pom holding the right of these *kopjes*, and were forced to retire, with a few casualties, Lieutenant Smith, of the Shropshire company, being seriously wounded, and taken prisoner. On learning that Lord Roberts was well on his way to Poplar Grove, the M.I. returned to their bivouac at Ferdinand's *kraal*, where they spent the night.

During the morning, two men of the Green Howards, Privates Wright and Bushby, behaved with great gallantry whilst on patrol. With 2nd-Lieutenant Tarbet, they had ridden up to a farm and were fired at at very short range. On this they retired, but Tarbet's horse fell over some barbed wire, throwing his rider, and leaving him with his foot caught in the stirrup. Private Wright rode back under a very heavy fire, and loosened the leather, upon which the horse bolted, but was caught by Bushby, thus enabling Tarbet to get away unhurt.

Colonel Henry forwarded these men's names to the brigadier for gallantry in the field.

On the 8th March, the 4th M.I. marched to Poplar Grove, and remained there till the 11th, when they went on to Petrusburg, as escort to a convoy. No more fighting occurred, and they reached Bloemfontein on the 17th March, and bivouacked about seven miles north of the town, at a Boer farm called Valambrosa.

Here they had an easy time of it for ten days, and were only called upon to do the ordinary camp duties, with an occasional patrol thrown in.

On the 31st, they marched to Roodeval, two miles south, where they joined the rest of their brigade, the 2nd and Burma M.I., under command of Colonel Martyr. The brigade then set forth in the direction of Sanna's Post, in order to cover Colonel Broadwood's retirement, who was known to be hard pressed, although no news had arrived of his disaster.

After marching about four miles in an easterly direction past Boesman's *kop*, the road bifurcated, one leading to the waterworks and the other going in a more westerly direction. Striking the Modder at Waterval *drift*, Colonel Martyr with the 2nd and Burma M.I., took the road to the waterworks, whilst Colonel Henry, supported by some Queensland M.I., made for Waterval *drift*.

On nearing the *drift*, the advance guard, comprising two sections of the Green Howards, rode up to occupy the high ground on the near side of the river. The Boers were seen moving about on the other side, but no firing took place. Colonel Henry then sent the Cornwall and Shropshire companies across the *drift*. They immediately occupied a long ridge on the far side of the river, and came into action.

Part of the Yorkshire company was on the Bloemfontein side of the *drift* and part on the right with 2nd-Lieutenant Nevile. The Boers were shelling our men on the far side, but the shrapnel was bursting too high, and many shells fell into the river. The Queensland M.I. were next sent across to reinforce the Cornwall and Shropshire, and lined the ridge to the left of them. After about an hour the Boers began to move round the left flank, so the Yorkshire half-company at the *drift* crossed the river, and came up on the left side of the Queenslanders. There was good cover among some rocks, and the men blazed away merrily, but were not nearly numerous enough to frustrate the Boers' turning movement. In about an hour's time, a retirement was ordered from the right, the half-company being, consequently, the last to leave.

It was about half-a-mile to the horses, which were reached without a casualty, but three of the Green Howards were wounded whilst crossing the *drift* as well as some horses.

By this time the 9th Division, ordered out from Bloemfontein as a reinforcement, had come up at about 4 p.m., and the Boers then cleared off.

Amongst other casualties in the 4th M.I. were Lieutenant Cantan and twenty men of the Cornwall company, who were taken prisoners.

A wretched night was spent by the outposts, no food or blankets, and a large force of the enemy in close proximity. By morning, however, they had departed, and the battalion, on being relieved at 8 a.m., bivouacked on the other side of the river. 2nd-Lieutenant Nevile had an eventful day. He was sent with a message to the waterworks, believed at the time to be held by our troops, but had to leave in a hurry when he found his mistake, with a large Boer patrol at his heels. On the 1st April the 9th Division marched back to Bloemfontein, with the 4th M.I. acting as rearguard, the latter eventually reaching their old camp at Valambrosa. On the 4th April they marched out to occupy Kranz Kraal wagon bridge over the Modder, about seven miles east of

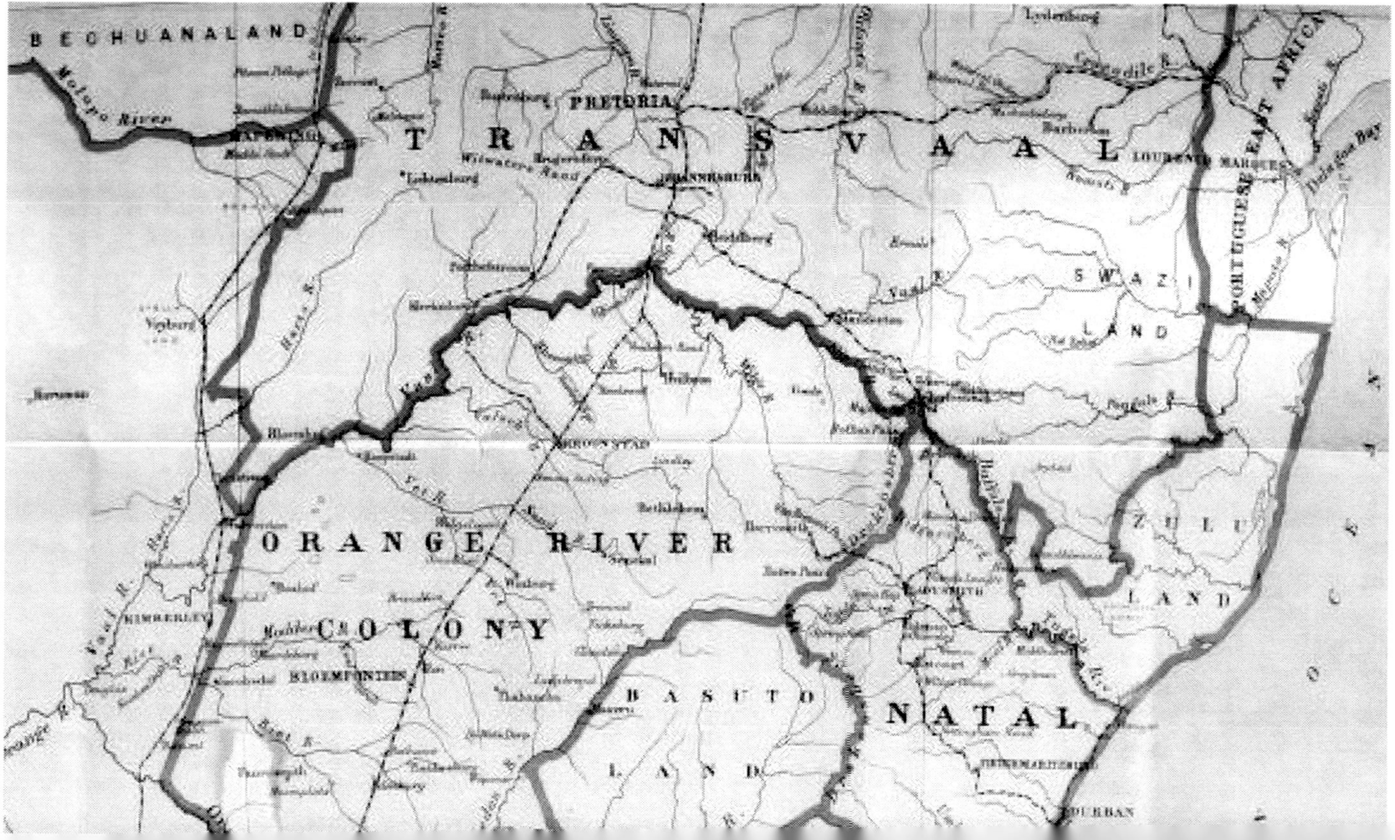
BECHUANALAND
TRANSVAAL
PRETORIA
JOHANNESBURG
SWAZI LAND
PORTUGUESE EAST AFRICA
ORANGE RIVER COLONY
BLOEMFONTEIN
KIMBERLEY
BASUTO LAND
NATAL
ZULU LAND
LADYSMITH
PIETERMARITZBURG
DURBAN
Molopo River
Crocodile R.
Delagoa Bay
Vaal R.
Lydenburg
Barberton
Heidelberg
Vryburg
Bethlehem
Harrismith

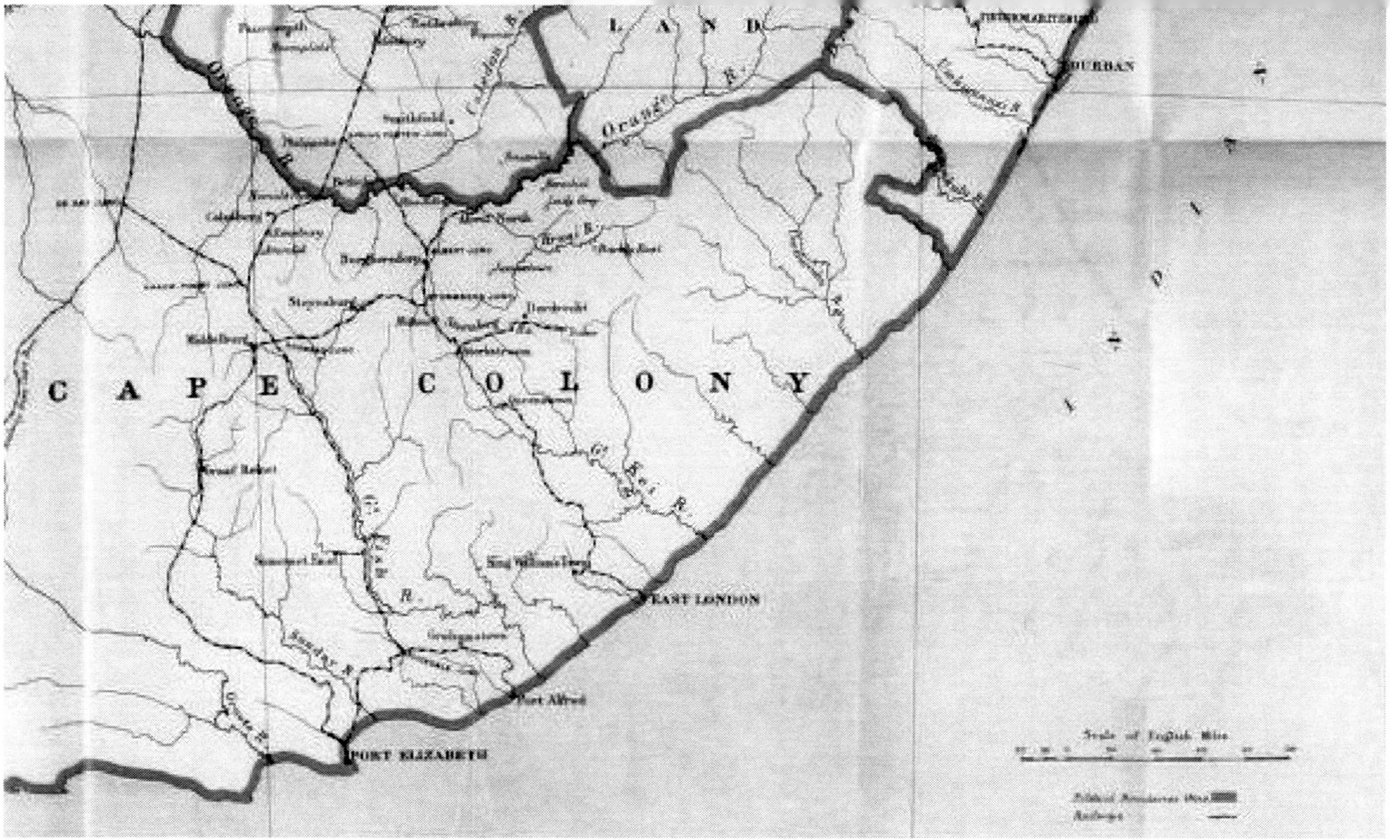
LAND
DURBAN
Orange R.
Caledon R.
CAPE COLONY
Dordrecht
Somerset East
King William's Town
EAST LONDON
Port Alfred
PORT ELIZABETH
Gt. Kei R.
Sundays R.
Scale of English Miles

the camp. The fit horses had by this time sadly diminished in number, and the whole regiment could only muster 120 mounted men.

On arriving, they were ordered back to Valambrosa, the position being considered to be too isolated to be held by so small a force.

On the 16th, camp was changed to Rusfontein about a mile and a half north of Bloemfontein, where a huge M.I. camp was being formed for the purpose of reorganising and refitting the whole of the M.I., imperial and colonial.

Colonel Henry was now given command of the 4th Corps, which was composed of the 4th M.I., the Victorian Mounted Rifles, the South Australian Mounted Rifles, and the Tasmanian M.I. Later on the 4th Corps was strengthened by the addition of a section of pom-poms and by J Battery R.H.A. Major Handcock took over command of the 4th M.I., *vice* Colonel Henry.

About this time the Royal Warwickshire company rejoined, having been away in the Prieska district all this time. They had had some fighting near Haudwater, and lost rather heavily.

On the 20th April, the corps received orders to march to Karee *kloof* beyond Karee siding, to take over the outpost line there, opposite the main Boer position in front of Brandfort. Karee *kloof* was a very comfortable place for a camp, and tents arrived for the men, which they had been without since January.

On the 23rd April, a large patrol, composed of men from every unit in the corps, moved out to make a demonstration in front of the Boers, whilst some movement on our right was taking place. A small patrol of the Yorkshire company was sent out to reconnoitre to the left front, and came under fire, and this was all that happened.

During the next week a few remounts arrived from Bloemfontein, all of them miserable crocks, so 2nd-Lieutenant Nevile was sent into Bloemfontein to try and get something better.

On the 30th April, the 4th Corps moved out beyond the outposts, and made a reconnaissance in force towards the enemy's position. The Victorians were on the extreme left, supported by the Cornwall and Warwickshire companies; on the right came the Green Howards, then the Shropshire, Tasmanians and Australians. On the right of all was part of the 8th Corps.

After advancing about a mile, the Boers were located beyond a low ridge, about 1,700 yards in front. The 4th M.I. immediately trotted on, and leaving their horses under cover of the ridge, came into action at once. Two pom-poms, under Captain Sterling, R.H.A., at once opened fire just on the left of the Yorkshire company with some effect, and then limbering up, moved to the left, near the Victorians, Cornwalls, and Warwickshire companies. The Boers immediately opened a heavy artillery fire on them, under which they were forced to retire, getting a terrible slating from the Boer riflemen, who had crept up within range under cover of their guns. The V.M.R. had several losses, including Captain Lilley, their Adjutant, shot in the head and captured, but the two companies of the 4th M.I. did not lose a man. The Boers then began shelling the M.I. and Lumsden's Horse on their right, killing several of the latter's led-horses. The M.I. then retired back to the next ridge, Lumsden's Horse losing very heavily through not withdrawing soon enough. Private Simpson, Yorkshire company, was hit, and had to be left, as he could not mount his horse. He was recovered a few days later when Brandfort was occupied.

The next day, the 1st May, General Maxwell's Brigade advanced and occupied Gun Hill without opposition. This was a large *kopje* about five miles north of the M.I. camp, and south-east of Brandfort, the strongest point in the Boer outpost line.

When the general advance began, the 4th Corps marched in the direction of Gun Hill, the remainder of the 7th Division just behind them; the 11th Division more to their left, leading straight on Brandfort itself.

About 8.30 p.m., word was received that the enemy were in full retreat, and the Yorkshire company pressed on as hard as their poor old Argentines could carry them over about a mile of flat, down and up a *donga*, and then up a high rocky ridge, behind which the horses were left. On descending on the other side, they were shelled all the way down. Here they had to wait till General Maxwell's brigade came up on their left. This infantry got badly shelled, and when level with the M.I., came in for a very hot rifle fire.

But the Boers were too much afraid of losing their artillery, and already their big gun was being hauled away. The whole of the 4th Corps was then brought up, and galloped to try and cut it off. The Boers were, however, too quick, and though they were followed till almost dark, the chase had to be given up, the M.I. retiring to their bivouac, about six miles south-east of Brandfort.

On the 5th May, the 4th Corps formed the advance guard. They were marching on the Vet River, and did not get sight of the Boers till they had ridden twenty miles, and then fought a rearguard action till dark. The next day the corps marched to Smaldeel junction, and from thence, the day following by a farm called Leuwkenil, about fifteen miles south of the Zand River. Here they rested on the 8th, during which 2nd-Lieutenant Nevile appeared on the scene with remounts. On the afternoon of the 9th they reached Biddulph farm, near Virginia siding, on the Zand River, where it was rumoured the enemy were going to make a desperate stand.

Before dawn, on the 10th, the mounted troops moved off. The 4th M.I.'s orders were to cross near Virginia siding and hold the far bank till the rest of the 4th Corps and the 3rd Cavalry Brigade had crossed.

Nevile, with half the Yorkshire company, were the first to gain the high ground on the other side, and came under a hot fire at first, till the battalion joined them, and then the Boers drew off. When the cavalry and guns came up, all advanced on both sides of the railway, the 4th M.I. keeping on the right of the line. The Boers did not attempt to stand, but fought a rearguard action all the time, blowing up the rails as they retreated.

The M.I. were not often within range of their rifle fire, but were shelled continuously till sunset, when they reached Ventersburg siding, about twenty-five miles all told.

Kroonstad was the next objective, thirty miles on. At noon the enemy were overtaken. They were posted on a strong line of *kopjes*. The 4th M.I. accordingly occupied some high ground about seventeen hundred yards from the enemy's position, whilst the horse artillery shelled the *kopjes*.

Desultory fire was kept up all day, but neither side could see much to fire at, as both had too good cover.

At sunset, strong picquets were posted along the ridge occupied all day, and the remainder of the M.I. withdrew to bivouac two miles in rear.

On the 12th, the army marched on Kroonstad, and presently heard that it had been evacuated during the night The 4th M.I. did not enter the town, but halted about two miles south, close to the bridge across the Valsch River, which the Boers had blown up the day before. Everyone expected to remain at Kroonstad and rest for a few days, and all needed it, especially the infantry.

On the 7th May, Lieutenant Stansfeld and twenty men joined the company from the regiment, and Nevile took over the duties of adjutant temporarily. Colonel Henry now assumed command of both the 4th and 8th Corps, the former being increased by the addition of J Battery R.H.A., under Major Enthoven.

On Tuesday, the 22nd May, the general advance on Pretoria began. The 4th M.I. started before daylight, and reached Wolverlaagte, seventeen miles, without coming in contact with the enemy.

On the 23rd, twenty miles were covered, taking them a little beyond Rhenoster Kop. The rails just here were blown up for quite two miles.

On the 24th, the Yorkshire company formed the right flank of the advance guard, and took three prisoners, besides a quantity of arms and ammunition.

This night, being the Queen's birthday, the men all got an issue of rum, and *God save the Queen* was sung by the whole of the force. It sounded very fine in the clear night air.

The next day they marched twenty-one miles to Wolvehoek, expecting a fight all day, as 4,000 Dutchmen were reported on their right flank; however, they remained on the right flank. The next *trek* was to Vereeniging, the first station across the Vaal. The Boers were said to be holding Viljoen's *drift*, village and colliery, about seventeen miles off. The 4th Corps was ordered to detain the enemy till the guns came up, and also to try and stop a trainload of *burghers* who were just leaving the station.

The 4th M.I. at once pressed on as fast as they could gallop, and arrived at the river just in time to prevent the Boers blowing up more than one span of the Vaal River bridge.

The Cornwall company thereupon occupied one of the mines south of the river, and began firing on a large number of the enemy, who had taken up a position on a coal mine on the far bank. These two mines were connected by telephone, and the manager in his office kept telling Captain Walker where his shots were going, and the strength and dispositions of the Boers. On the remainder of the battalion coming up, the 4th M.I. were the first troops across the Vaal on the 26th May. The whole battalion was on outpost duty the same night, occupying the positions vacated by the enemy. Captain Walker was now in command, as Major Handcock was down with fever, and did not again take an active part in the operations till the 1st June.

The 11th Division, with the headquarter staff, did not arrive till about noon the next day, and the 4th Corps then pushed on along the Vaal River to support General Gordon and the Lancer Brigade, who were reported to be held up in a bend of the river. But they were never found, as they had never been there, and much time was wasted looking for them. Three men of the Warwick company were taken prisoners on the left flank. The corps spent a wretched night, as it was bitterly cold, for no transport had turned up, and the men were, consequently, without either blankets or food.

Next morning, Klip River station was reached, where there was a farm and plenty of forage. The horses had a good feed, which they wanted badly, having had nothing worth speaking of for two days.

Moving on again on the 29th, the 4th M.I. were ordered to seize the junction of the Natal and Free State lines, as it was reported that two trains full of *burghers* were coming up from Natal. Captain Walker, D.C.L.I., immediately took the regiment forward at a trot, and after going about six miles, a ridge was reached, and the two trains were seen standing still about a mile distant. Long-range volleys were at once opened, whereupon a great number of Boers left the trains to hold an adjacent *kopje*, the trains in the meantime starting off again.

The regiment advanced slowly, and sweeping round to the right of the *kopje*, galloped on to seize another position about a mile further, overlooking Boksburg, being shelled by the enemy as they proceeded. A halt was made here for two hours, and a heavy fire was exchanged with some of the enemy advancing from Germiston. Lieutenant-Colonel Ross, commanding the 8th Corps, was with the 4th M.I. at this time, and they were also much helped by a Colt battery. The Boers finally drew off to the hills north of Germiston, and Boksburg was thereupon occupied. Colonel Ross then ordered Captain Walker to take about 20 men and seize Elandsfontein station at all costs. So accompanied by Lieutenants Stansfeld and Nevile and twenty-three men of the Green Howards, he started off at a gallop for Elandsfontein. On their arrival there, they dismounted, and, fixing bayonets, they dashed into the station. There was a hospital train with two engines just leaving for Pretoria and another filled with rifles and entrenching tools. Both of these were stopped, and all the officials made prisoners. On learning that a train full of Boers was expected from Johannesburg at 11 a.m., an engine was sent with two men to pull up a rail, so as to stop its arrival at Elandsfontein.

There must have been a good many Boers near the station, for when they realised that there was only a small party there, they began sniping from all the buildings close by. On the arrival of the 4th Corps they cleared off, and the battalion spent an uncomfortable, but unmolested, night a mile beyond Elandsfontein, being without blankets or food of any description.

The battalion was congratulated in army orders by the commander-in-chief for its work on the above occasion. The 4th Corps rested on the 30th, and, resuming their march on the 31st, halted at the waterworks near Johannesburg, and picquetted the Pretoria road whilst the army marched through the town. The Yorkshire company, in spite of being on picquet, had a fairly good time, both officers and men being hospitably entertained by some Scotch people in a neighbouring house.

The same night the 4th M.I. bivouacked beyond Orange Grove, on the Pretoria road, about six miles north-east of Johannesburg. Remaining there for two days, the advance continued on the 3rd June, and the next day the Boers were met with at Six-Mile *spruit*. The Cornwall company were acting as advanced guard, and had rather a warm reception, and had to be reinforced by the Green Howards. Soon the whole corps came up and seized a long ridge beyond the *spruit* The Boers continued to retreat, and an advance was made to another ridge. Here they were joined by J Battery, which eventually succeeded in silencing the Boer guns. The ridge was then handed over to the 11th Division, the 4th Corps moved off to make a turning movement on left flank.

On the 5th, after the surrender, the whole army, except the modest 4th M.I., marched past Lord Roberts in Market Square. The regiment meanwhile bivouacked in a salubrious spot, called Dead Horse Nullah, and did not *trek* again till the 7th, when it marched to Silverton.

Passing the 11th Division on their way, the M.I. went to Erste Fabrieken, and were about to settle down there when they were shelled by a Long Tom placed on a railway track at Peinaar's Poort, about 11,000 yards off. So a less dangerous place had to be selected for their camp. The battalion remained halted on the 9th, but sent out a strong reconnoitring party, under Captain Walker, in the direction of Edendale

On Sunday, the 10th, Lieutenant Stansfeld went out with twenty men in the same direction. The Boers laid a trap to catch them on their return, but they all got clear with the exception of Private Rose (Yorkshire company), who, unfortunately, was taken prisoner.

For the next three days the battalion occupied a spot near Edendale. In the meantime the battle of Diamond Hill was being fought, and on the enemy retiring on Bronkhorst *spruit*, the battalion moved to Donkershoek, where it remained till the 23rd, doing constant patrolling and picquet work, daily expecting an attack.

On the 22nd June, Lieutenant Stansfeld escorted envoys from General Botha to Pretoria to confer with Lord Roberts as to peace terms, but nothing came of this, as De Wet had in the meanwhile obtained some signal successes, which gave the Boers, for the time, more heart.

On the 23rd, the Guards' Brigade relieved the 4th M.I at Donkershoek, the latter returning to Peinaar's Poort. Here there was a good deal of patrolling to be done, and though the battalion never lost any men, the Victoria Mounted Rifles were not so lucky, and had one man killed and two taken prisoners on the 5th July. Private Robinson (Yorkshire company) had his horse shot when out with Lieutenant Underwood (Shropshire company), and Private Pepper had his rifle shot out of his hand near Vandermerve station. A week later the battalion was ordered to occupy a ridge of *kopjes* between Derdepoort and Erste Fabrieken, and on the 17th July, returned once more to Peinaar's Poort

Just before the general advance eastwards, Captain Holmes took over command of the Yorkshire company, *vice* Major Handcock, who was appointed to command the regiment on Colonel Henry being given the 4th Corps.

The advance commenced on the 23rd July, and was continued each day till the 27th, when a halt was made at Brugspruit, where the leading brigade of the 11th Division had come to a standstill

The 4th M.I. was now split up all along the line between Bronkhorst *spruit* and Groot Oliphant's River, the Green Howards' company going to Balmoral, where their own regiment happened to be stationed.

Here the patrols often came in contact with the enemy north of the line, and Private Varlow, when out with Lieutenant Nevile, was killed in a skirmish on the 12th August. On another occasion, Colour-Sergeant Parkinson was out in charge of six men. He got in touch with a large body of Boers, who chased the little party back towards the station. One of the horses was dead beat, and its owner would have been captured had not Colour-Sergeant Parkinson dismounted, and, under a heavy fire, got his comrade up on his own horse, and all managed to get away. Some of the Boers got within 100 yards, and it was only by great luck that the patrol got in without losing a man. For this act, as well as for gallantry on other occasions, Colour-Sergeant Parkinson was awarded the Distinguished Conduct Medal.

The company remained at Balmoral till about the middle of August, and on the general advance being resumed, the whole of the 4th Corps concentrated at Wonderfontein on the 23rd, previous to attacking the Boers, who were in a strong position near Belfast, twelve miles distant.

On the 24th, the whole force, which included the 11th Division, started off with this object The 4th M.I. kept to the railway till they came to some rising ground, from which could be seen Belfast and the monument beyond. Here the 4th Corps wheeled to the left in order to make a turning movement, whilst the 11th Division marched straight on the town. The ground traversed was very rough going, and it was not till close on 2 p.m. that the Yorkshire and Cornwall companies, who constituted the advance guard, began to swing round to the right and make towards Monument hill.

On reaching a ridge north of this they at once came under fire, and during the hour they occupied it, three or four men were hit and several horses. Orders were now received to hold Monument hill, and the two companies advanced under a heavy fire to the top, where they remained till nearly dusk. Several more men were hit here, and the Warwick company, who were further to the right, had also several casualties.

The Yorkshire company had five men wounded, and Lieutenant Tarbet was for the second time hit in the wrist. Just as it was getting dark, the Royal Warwickshire Regiment relieved these three companies, who spent a bitterly cold night, with no food or blankets, as the transport had not appeared.

After the operations at Belfast, the 4th M.I. went north, and passing through Helvetia on 30th August, picquetted the hills above Waterval-onder for several days. On 6th September, the corps marched to Machadodorp, and on the 9th, advanced on Weltevreden. The Green Howards and Cornwall companies, under Captains Holmes and Walker, constituted the advance guard, and at 10 a.m. came in touch with the Boers, who were holding a ridge just north of Weltevreden farm. A pom-pom which was with these two companies, was taken too close up, and three horses of the Shropshire company, under 2nd-Lieutenant Hooper, were shot before it could get away. The two companies advanced under cover of J Battery, R.H.A., and seized a *kopje* on the right of the Boer position. About noon, being reinforced by the 1st Corps, the enemy's left was turned, and they beat a hasty retreat. The official casualty list of the Boers showed twenty-two killed, the 4th M.I. losses being entirely confined to horses. They were ad-

MEDALS AND CLASPS AWARDED TO THE BATTALION AND TO THE 4TH M.I.

dressed by General Hutton the same evening, who thanked them for their services, and especially complimented Captain Walker for what had been done in the day's fight.

After the engagement at Weltevreden, the battalion remained in bivouac in the neighbourhood of Waterval-boven and Waterval-onder.

The cavalry division was on its way to Barberton, General Buller's force was marching from Helvetia to Lydenburg, whither a large portion of the Boer army had retreated, and the 11th Division was halted between Helvetia and Waterval-onder.

A large number of the enemy, including the vast majority of the foreign contingent, were at the same time *trekking* along the Delagoa railway towards Komati Poort, not to mention Kruger himself in his railway carriage. To the 11th Division, therefore, to which the 4th Corps formed the mounted troops, fell the task of advancing on Komati Poort, and at the same time occupying the Delagoa Bay railway.

The corps marched to Uitkomst on the 7th September, and the next day to Kaapsche Hoop, which was reached after two days, over a very rough country. It was quite impassable for any wheeled transport except the lightest of carts, so that most of the guns and wagons went down the Nooigedacht valley with the infantry.

A few days later the Guards' Brigade marched up from Godwaan station, and together with the 4th Corps, pushed on to Jamestown, in the Kaap valley, and then on to Avoca, passing by Kaapmuiden junction.

Komati Poort was reached by the end of September, and although the Boers were not met with all this time, and there was no fighting, the 4th M.I. have reason for not forgetting this period. The men were on siege rations, except as regards meat, which was to be had in plenty of the *trek* ox variety; the horses had no rations or forage at all, and existed (those that did exist) on the little that could be got in the shape of *mealies*, there being no grazing worth mentioning.

The total strength of the regiment as it marched into Komati Poort was sixty-six mounted men. The Warwick company was away, having been left for patrol duty at Waterval-onder.

The following account of the entry of the troops into Komati Poort is taken from O *Futuro*, a paper published at Delagoa Bay:

> When the sun rose on Monday morning the only living things to be seen in Komati Poort were a small boy and his dog. But at ten minutes past seven a man in khaki suddenly appeared from behind one of the houses. A minute after another was

seen, then two more, and one man riding one horse and leading some others across the open space by the railway station. And for more than an hour these men of the Yorkshire company M.I. held the town entirely by themselves, visiting house after house and disarming a few Boers found lurking about At half-past eight a little cloud of dust could be seen rising about eight or nine miles away beyond Oorsprong. Then, as the cloud came nearer and increased in size, two men could be seen in front, then other twos on the flanks quickly followed by a company in extended order, and after them the supports, and gradually out of the cloud the main body of the division was evolved. It was a magnificent sight to watch the deploying of the column, company after company, battalion after battalion, taking position on either side of the town, filling the town itself, and then lining the river. At ten o'clock the first big gun passed the railway station, and a few minutes afterwards a machine gun was placed in position to command the bridge, and then six men took their lives in their hands and crossed the bridge, not knowing one instant from another but what they would be blown to atoms from the expected explosion, for it was well known that the bridge had been mined by the Boers, and it was thought that they would take the opportunity of blowing it up while the troops were upon it. But to the relief of all who witnessed it, the little party got safely over, and others soon followed. The first men to cross were Captain Holmes and Lieutenant Stansfeld, of the Yorkshire company 4th Regt. Mounted Infantry, shortly followed by Lieutenant Nevile, and these are the first officers who have marched right through the Transvaal from border to border. Our correspondent had the pleasure of welcoming them, and taking them over the frontier with the permission of the Portuguese commandant, who arrived on the scene just after the officers reached the summit of the hill, and subject to their leaving their arms with their men on the Transvaal side. The two first-named officers did this, and descended the hill to Ressano Garcia. From here a start was made to return to the British camp along the railway line. Here the hasty departure of the Boers was very strongly in evidence. Dozens of tents had been left standing, still furnished with chairs, tables, bedsteads, and, in some cases, even the clocks were still hanging to the tent poles, food was on the tables, and many of the English Tommies who were sent to guard the line rejoiced in enjoying what their 'Brother Boer' had so hurriedly left behind. But soon sterner evidences of war were met with. Thousands of Martini-Henry cartridges with the murderous soft-nosed bullet, Mauser cartridges for rifle and pistol, coated with a suspicious-looking green grease, cases for pom-pom shells, and very many Long Tom shells, filled and ready to do their deadly work. But the most curious thing of all were several hundred hand grenades. What the Boers intended doing with these it is most difficult to say, as they have not been in the habit of getting sufficiently close to the British soldier to pitch a hand grenade at him. For nearly half-a-mile the line was strewn on either side with coffee, sugar and flour, a lot of it burning and hundreds of bags ripped open and contents oozing out. Valuable telegraphic instruments, saddles, bridles, and books enough to stock a Bunyan's miscellaneous store.

A few days later information was received that a large Boer convoy was *trekking* away due north, almost parallel to and close to the Selati railway, and a force of mounted men was ordered to follow it. By dint of picking out the fittest horses in the whole of the 4th Corps, a column of 200 rifles paraded under Captain Walker. It was composed of fifty of the 4th M.I. under Captain White, and the remainder were made up of contingents from the Australian and Tasmanian Rifles. In addition, there were two guns from J Battery and a pom-pom.

A track was followed through the bush, and along the Selati railway, parallel to the line of advance were fifty of Captain Steinacker's Irregulars. The latter had charge of supplies for the expedition, excepting two days' rations and forage, carried on the horses. To cut a long story short, the column marched ninety miles through dense bush country, but did not get touch with the convoy, nor was anything more seen of Steinacker and the rations, and finally the force marched back to Komati, where it arrived on the 4th October. The horses, on the return journey, simply died in batches from nothing else but sheer starvation; at least fifty were lost out of the 200.

The 11th Division was now broken up, and the headquarters of the 4th M.I. went by rail to Pretoria, leaving, as part of the garrison at Komati, the Green Howards' company and the Shropshire, the horses of the Cornwall company and the Australians being handed over to them.

Major-General Hutton, who had commanded the whole of the 1st Brigade (four corps), was now sent home to take up a colonial appointment, and the whole of the M.I. in South Africa came under the command of Colonel Alderson. At the same time, Major Handcock, who had commanded the 4th M.I. for the past six months, was appointed to the command of the M.I. depot at Pretoria, and Captain Walker was given the command of the regiment with the local rank of Major.

Before attempting to describe the work which the 4th M.I. was called upon to do during the remainder of the campaign, the following list of the officers with the various companies at this time may be of interest:

Commanding Officer: Major H. B. Walker, Duke of Cornwall's Light Infantry. Adjutant: Lieutenant W. G. Tarbet, P.W.O. Yorkshire Regiment. The Warwick company (at Waterval-onder).—Captain C. Christie (who had just relieved Captain Toogood, invalided), Lieutenants Methuen and Moffat. The Yorkshire company (at Komati Poort).—Captain H. G. Holmes, Lieutenants Liddon (joined at Komati Poort), Stansfeld and Nevile. The Cornwall company (at Pretoria with headquarters).— Lieutenants Romilly, Stericker, and 2nd-Lieutenant Kingston. Captain Stokoe joined the company to command a few weeks later. The Shropshire company (at Komati Poort).—Captain White, Lieutenants Underwood, Fitzgerald and Hooper. Lieutenant H. M. Smith rejoined shortly afterwards from England, and on Captain White being invalided, took over command of the company. The companies numbered about 100 non-commissioned officers and men, having been strengthened by drafts from the four line battalions.

Early in November the headquarters left Pretoria for Kaapsche Hoop, where they were joined by the Green Howards' company, and remained there till the 24th January, when they went to Machadodorp. All this time they had detachments at Komati, Barberton and Waterval-boven. In December, Captain Holmes left, on his appointment to command the 15th M.I.

The mounted men (there were a great many dismounted at the time) left Kaapsche Hoop first. Most of these belonged to the Shropshire company, but there were some of the Green Howards, under Lieutenant Liddon, half being left at Kaapsche Hoop with Lieutenant Nevile. On their way they were commandeered by Colonel Henry, and did not rejoin headquarters till May. They took part in the operations under General French, and *trekked* all over the country, as far as

Newcastle, Amsterdam and Piet Retief. They formed part of the column, under Major-General Smith-Dorrien, when it was attacked at Lake Chrissie, and in a fight near Piet Retief in February, Lieutenant Fitzgerald (S.L.I.) was badly wounded in the leg.

Till about the middle of February all the troops on the eastern line had been sitting down on the railway, the consequence being that nearly every station between Machadodorp and Middleburg had been attacked, the line at various points torn up, and trains wrecked.

The largest, in fact, the main body of the enemy north of the line, were about 2,000 strong, and had their headquarters at Dullstroom. They were under Ben Viljoen and Muller, were all good fighting men, well mounted and energetic, and had proved themselves such by their vigorous attacks at Machadodorp, Belfast, and the capture of the Helvetia garrison.

Accordingly, Brigadier-General Walter Kitchener was ordered to break up Viljoen's force, and with a column composed of 1,300 infantry and 500 mounted men, left Helvetia on the 11th February with this object. The Boers were met with close to Dullstroom, and being in superior numbers to the column, it was deemed advisable to draw back into Belfast. A rearguard action was fought till within ten miles of Belfast, and on the column being reinforced by a squadron of the 19th Hussars and some of the 4th M.I., the enemy drew off to Dullstroom. Captain Crichton (Manchester Regiment) was killed, and amongst about 20 casualties, there was Lieutenant Cameron (Warwick company) and one of his men wounded.

From the 24th January until July, 1901, the Yorkshire company remained split up, the party, under Lieutenant Liddon, being away till May, and the two sections with Lieutenant Nevile at Kaapsche Hoop, did not rejoin headquarters till the beginning of July.

During the above period the battalion was employed in convoy duty, patrolling the railway and picquetting the line to protect trains. Towards the end of March it joined a column under General Walter Kitchener, and swept the Komati valley as far as the Carolina road, bringing in large numbers of cattle, and being frequently engaged with the enemy.

From the 29th March to the 7th April the battalion remained at Machadodorp, finding escorts for convoys, in addition to the ordinary picquet and patrol work. Between this date and the first week in May they were attached to a column under Colonel Park, which, in connection with another under Brigadier-General Kitchener, was operating in the northern Transvaal under direction of General Bindon Blood. A good deal of fighting took place, but the section of the Green Howards under Lieutenant Stansfeld, do not appear to have had any casualties.

After the column was broken up, the 4th M.I. occupied the line between Peinaar's Poort and Machadodorp, a distance of 100 miles, the Green Howards taking the section between Brugspruit and Witbank. About this time Captain Hartley joined, and took over command of the company, which was now augmented by Lieutenant Liddon's party, and very shortly afterwards by Lieutenant Nevile's two sections from Kaapsche Hoop. All the other detachments had come in, and on the 4th July were at Wonderfontein, from whence they started north with a column under Brigadier-General Spens, for the purpose of clearing the country up the Steelpoort valley, the work consisting of removing Boer families from their farms, collecting stock and supplies, and destroying the farmsteads.

On the 13th July, a return convoy was sent back to the line under Major Rhodes, Royal Berkshire Regiment, being escorted by Lieutenant Nevile and twenty men, partly 4th M.I. and partly 5th Lancers.

The convoy halted for the night at Sterk-*loop*. Just before dark information came that some Boers, with several wagons and cattle were going into *laager* about six miles away. Nevile at once saddled up, and coming up to the *laager*, galloped it, taking the Boers completely by surprise. For this action he was specially promoted some months later.

Marching from Blinkwater, the 4th M.I. were at Honing's Kloof on the 12th July, having made a night march, when they captured fifteen prisoners and much sheep and cattle.

A few days later, near Klipplaats *drift*, Lieutenant Liddon with ten men were on the left flank, and succeeded in driving some Boers into the advance guard of the Yorkshire company, who killed one, wounded one, and took one prisoner, the M.I. casualties being two men wounded, and two horses killed. Marching by Doornkop, the column reached Middleburg on the 20th July.

The regiment was now ordered to join Colonel Park's command at Dullstroom, and arrived there, escorting a large convoy, on the 27th. Operations took place at once, and Captain Hartley, who was in command, on the 30th July came across the Boers near Witpoort, where they were in a very strong position. The men were ordered to dismount, and led by Captain Hartley, rushed the position, the enemy not waiting to be accosted. Two men of the Green Howards were wounded in this affair. On the way back to camp the rearguard were kept busy, and it was not till nearly dark that the enemy drew off on the arrival of two guns and the rest of the column.

After much *trekking* in the vicinity of Rossenekal, the 4th M.I. were sent to reinforce Brigadier-General Kitchener's column, which was rounding up Viljoen's commando, and arrived at Rooi Kraals on the 9th August The operations lasted a week, and were not very satisfactory.

Returning to Colonel Park's column, the battalion for the next few days traversed no new country. At Honing's *kloof* a Boer hospital was discovered, containing eleven wounded. They were taken away by the column, which returned to Middleburg on the 11th September to re-equip and to draw remounts, for the mountainous district in which they had been operating had been very hard on the horses. This being accomplished, the column marched to Lydenburg, which was reached by the end of the month.

Moving out from Lydenburg at 6 p.m. on 2nd of October, the 4th M.I. formed the advanced guard with the Manchester Regiment as main body, and crossing the Spekboom River, made for Oliphant's Poort On emerging from the pass, a halt was made at De Grootboom farm so as to allow the infantry to come up. Pushing on up the Pilgrim's Rest coach road, the M.I. were to endeavour to occupy the heights overlooking the town. The men dismounted, and when within 100 yards of the crest the darkness was lit up by the flashes from the enemy's rifles, who were firing into the led horses, which were then being retired. They did not wait for the men who were crawling up, but decamped straight away. The M.I. had five men wounded, three of whom were Green Howards, thirteen horses killed and wounded, and about a dozen men badly hurt from falls.

The next day or two was spent clearing the Origstad valley, and on the 4th October, when going back to camp, information was received that 150 Boers were coming down a *donga* on the right flank. Lieutenant Liddon was sent down with a company to hold it till the rearguard had crossed, and while doing so he was badly wounded in the thigh. Lieutenant Stansfeld had a narrow escape, a bullet smashing his cigarette case, whilst he came off without injury.

The Boer families and the wounded were now escorted halfway back to Lydenburg. On the 6th October, Major Walker, who had taken over the command from Captain Hartley, descended into the Origstad valley to surround certain farms before dawn, the infantry and guns being posted on the heights above. On reaching Rosenkrantz farm, on the road to Pilgrim's Rest, they suddenly came under fire from a neighbouring *kopje*, when Captain Stokoe (Cornwall company) and 2nd-Lieutenant Crooke (Warwick company) were both severely wounded, and there were several other casualties amongst the men and horses. The Warwick company, supported by the Green Howards, immediately galloped the *kopje*, and pushed on about two miles along the valley, fighting a rearguard action back to camp.

On the 7th, the column marched back to Lydenburg, arriving there two days later. There the 4th M.I. remained till the 18th of December, the Green Howards being reinforced by a draft of twenty men from the 21st M.I. during this period. Lieutenant Morgan, from the 1st Battalion, and Lieutenants Bagley and Clegg, from the 4th Battalion, also joined them at Lydenburg.

The column was now ordered to Dullstroom, where there was a small commando hovering about, and when camped at Elandspruit were attacked by the enemy at about 9 p.m., who opened a heavy fire from the south side.

The Manchester Regiment held the *kopjes* on the west, the 4th M.I. the south and east, and some National Scouts were on the north side.

The first attack was probably a feint, for a number of the enemy were crawling up in the darkness on to the Manchester Regiment, who were heavily engaged. Luckily, the moon was rising; the attack was beaten off, and was not again renewed. At daybreak twenty-two dead Boers were picked up, in addition to four wounded. The column had fifteen killed and seventeen wounded, the majority belonging to the Manchester Regiment.

The 4th M.I. now marched into Machadodorp and on to Belfast, where they remained till the 16th January.

Up to the 29th of January they operated with Colonel Park's and Colonel Urmston's columns in the country round Dullstroom, when they returned to Lydenburg. There they stayed till the 11th of February, when they marched through the Badfontein valley to Machadodorp, thence along the railway to Pan, which was reached a week later.

On the 19th February, Colonel Park's column, assisted by Colonel Williams' Australians, made a night march north of Pan, and covered thirty odd miles before daybreak. Their objective was Jack Hindon's and Karl Trichart's commandos on the Bothasberg.

Complete success attended the march. The 4th M.I. galloped the *laager* at dawn, completely surprising the Boers. The result was 164 prisoners and eight Boers killed and wounded, 100 horses, 630 cattle, and large quantities of rifles and ammunition. Some of the prisoners were caught by Colonel Williams' column, into which the 4th M.I. had driven them. Hindon managed to escape.

Marching back to Belfast, 200 men of the 4th M.I., which included sixty of the Green Howards, entrained on the 27th February for Bronkhorst *spruit*, their object being to attack Schalk Burgher's *laager*, which was near Rhenoster Kop, some thirty miles north-west of the station. They reached the spot about 6 a.m. on the 28th of February, and surprised the *laager*, capturing altogether seventeen prisoners. The M.I. spent the night at Rhenoster Kop, having covered seventy miles in eighteen hours.

From 11th to 16th of March the whole of Colonel Park's column were operating in the vicinity of Rhenoster Kop, and captured a few prisoners as well as stock. On the night of the 11th March and during the day of the 12th, the 4th M.I. marched eighty miles, and the infantry (Manchester Regiment) just under forty. The horses stood this long march wonderfully well, and there was not a sore back in the regiment

From the 17th March to the 29th April, the 4th M.I. were constantly on the move, working between the Delagoa and Natal lines, drawing supplies from stations near Middleburg one week, and from those near Standerton the next They took part in all the *drives* under General Bruce Hamilton, their column being strengthened most of the time by the 8th Hussars.

Early in May they returned to their old hunting ground round about Dullstroom, the last fight they had being a rearguard action on the 12th, when retiring on Belfast from Swartz *kopjes*.

The Yorkshire company left the regiment on the 9th August, when it was stationed at Middleburg, and joined their line battalion at Elandsfontein prior to its departure for England.

That the 4th M.I. should be broken up at the end of the war was inevitable. Of the four regiments represented in its ranks, one, the 2nd Royal Warwickshire, had already left South Africa; the Green Howards were under orders for England; the 2nd King's Shropshire Light Infantry expected to go to India, and the Duke of Cornwall's Light Infantry hoped to leave the country by the end of the year. A considerable number of men from each of the above-named battalions had served together in the 4th M.I. since January, 1900, and loyal as they were to their own regiments, there had grown up to be a great- *esprit de corps* in the 4th M.I. From being a unit, composed of men drawn from four different regiments, they had become a regiment themselves in the true sense of the word, and more than justified their existence, as did all the old M.I. regiments raised at the beginning of the war. Consequently, the break-up of the corps was felt by all more than can be imagined.

It is difficult, in a short narrative such as this, to do justice to its doings, but it is hoped that what has now been written may serve to keep green the memory of the old 4th M.I. in South Africa.

Appendices

APPENDIX A.

Names of Officers and Colour-Sergeants of the Green Howards who embarked on board the S.S. "Doune Castle."

Lieutenant-Colonel H. Bowles .. .. Commanding Officer.
Major J. A. Fearon .. .. .. Second in Command.
Captain G. Christian .. .. Adjutant.
Captain C. Organ .. .. Quarter-Master.
Sergeant-Major A. J. Hughes.
Quarter-Master-Sergeant S. Eastwood.
Orderly-Room-Sergeant C. Watmuff.

Company Officers and Colour-Sergeants.

"A" Captain M. L. Ferrar, Lieutenant R. H. Darwin, 2nd-Lieutenant W. G. Tarbet, Colour-Sergeant E. Pickard.

"B" Captain E. Somervell, 2nd-Lieutenant M. M. H. Nevile, Colour-Sergeant B. Williams.

"C" Major G. C. S. Handcock, Lieutenant C. F. C. Jarvis, 2nd-Lieutenant E. S. Broun, Colour-Sergeant W. Thirkell.

"D" Captain M. H. Orr, Colour-Sergeant F. Roberts.

"E" Major T. D. Kirkpatrick, 2nd-Lieutenant T. W. Stansfeld, Colour-Sergeant J. Robinson.

"F" Captain G. Pearson, 2nd-Lieutenant E. V. L. Wardle, Colour-Sergeant W. Weare.

"G" Captain E. M. Esson, 2nd-Lieutenant C. H. de St. P. Bunbury, Colour-Sergeant J. Walker.

"H" Captain B. C. W. Williams, Colour-Sergeant W. Bryant.

Medical Officer in Charge.

Major N. C. Ferguson, R.A.M.C.

March of the 6th Division from Enslin-Graspan to Bloemfontein.

12th February to 14th March, 1900.

Date.	From.	To.	Hour of Start.	Hour of Arrival.	Distance. Miles
Feb. 12	Enslin-Graspan	Ramdam	6 a.m.	1 p.m.	9¼
,, 13	Ramdam	Waterval Drift	5 a.m.	11 a.m.	10
,, 14	Waterval Drift	Wegdrai	1 a.m.	11 a.m.	9¼
,, 14	*a* Wegdrai	Klip Drift	5 p.m.	12.30 a.m. 15th	11½
,, 16	} *b* Klip Drift	Brandvallei	5 a.m.	12 noon 17th	} 11
,, 17			3 a.m.	12.30 p.m.	
,, 17	*c* Brandvallei	Paardeberg	5 p.m.	9.30 p.m.	4¼
,, 18	*d* Paardeberg	Boer Laager	3 a.m.	7 a.m.	1¾
Mar. 1	*e* Boer Laager	Osfontein	9.30 a.m.	11.30 a.m.	4
,, 7	*f* Osfontein	Poplar Grove	3.30 a.m.	7 p.m.	20
,, 8	*g* Poplar Grove	Roodepoort Farm	12 noon	4.30 p.m.	7
,, 10	*h* Roodepoort Farm	Driefontein (near)	6 a.m.	6 p.m.	10
,, 11	Driefontein	Kaals Spruit Farm	5.30 a.m.	3 p.m.	14
,, 12	Kaals Spruit Farm	Venters Vallei	5.30 a.m.	2.30 p.m.	12½
,, 13	*i* Venters Vallei	Brand Kop	3 p.m.	1 a.m. 14th	13¾
,, 14	*k* Brand Kop	Bloemfontein	9 a.m.	2 p.m.	6

(*a*) Affair with enemy's outposts.
(*b*) 13th Brigade engaged with enemy's rearguard, 18th Brigade followed.
(*c*) 55¾ miles in five marching days.
(*d*) Battle of Paardeberg.
(*e*) Change Camp.
(*f*) Including detour.
(*g*) Drove enemy from positions.
(*h*) Battle of Driefontein.
(*i*) 77 miles in six days, 7th to 13th.
(*k*) March through Bloemfontein.

APPENDIX B.

CASUALTIES.

KILLED IN ACTION, SLINGERSFONTEIN, CAPE COLONY, 15TH JANUARY, 1900.

3416	Col.-Sergt. F. Roberts.		5561 Private A. Smith.	
5156	Sergeant D. Jamieson.		3149 ,, B. Duffy.	
	2435 Private E. Ward.			

WOUNDED AT SLINGERSFONTEIN, 15TH JANUARY, 1900.

Captain M. H. Orr, (body and hand).

3992	Private J. Biggs.		818 Private F. Evans.	
2919	,, S. Clough.		5914 ,, C. Flood.	
	3423 Private J. Hayes.			

WOUNDED NEAR KLIP DRIFT, ORANGE FREE STATE, 16TH FEBRUARY, 1900.

2nd-Lieutenant W. G. Tarbet, 4th M.I., (wrist).
2384 Private W. Hamley, 4th M.I.

KILLED AT PAARDEBERG, ORANGE FREE STATE, 18TH FEBRUARY, 1900.

2nd-Lieutenant A. C. Neave.

3920	Col.-Sergt.	P. Hughes.	766	Private	T. Langan †
3160	Sergeant	R. Tate.	3356	,,	J. McHale.†
3231	Corporal	J. H. Kearns.	5003	,,	W. Mulligan.
1233	,,	T. Frankland.	3637	,,	H. Newton.†
4684	Lc.-Cpl.	D. Horton.	2258	,,	O. O'Shaughnessy.†
2831	Private	J. Brown.	3224	,,	A. Robinson.
2815	,,	F. Carley.	762	,,	H. Royston.
3210	,,	C. Chaplin.	3174	,,	G. Smith.
1103	Bandsman	T. W. Davis.	2544	,,	G. Sowerby.†
2613	Private	W. Diplock.	4847	,,	R. W. Tinkler.
2579	,,	S. Greetham.	2593	,,	T. Trinder.
4833	,,	C. Harrison.	5823	,,	F. Turvey.
5254	,,	E. Horton.	1264	,,	W. Ward.
5677	,,	H. Johnson.	4913	,,	J. Watson.
3422	,,	F. Jones.	3119	,,	J. Webb.

WOUNDED AT PAARDEBERG, 18TH FEBRUARY, 1900.

Lieutenant-Col. H. Bowles, (severely, chest).
Major T. D. Kirkpatrick (dangerously, neck).
Captain A. C. Buckle, (S. Staffordshire Rgt., attached, dangerously, neck).
Lieutenant C. V. Edwards, (severely, knee).

3264	Sergeant	A. Atkinson.*	2328	Private	R. Hand.
2898	Corporal	J. Collins.	3039	,,	H. Harrison.
1319	,,	J. Henderson.	5551	,,	J. Hellings.
4633	,,	G. H. King.	1671	,,	A. Hopwood.†
5267	,,	W. Stalker.	398	,,	W. Ingleson.
4916	,,	W. Wiles.	5946	,,	J. Jefferson.
4503	Lc.-Cpl.	J. Barrett.	5905	,,	T. Kielty.
5818	,,	J. Dullingham.*	5781	,,	J. Kennedy.
5684	,,	A. Hatton.	5055	,,	J. Lilly.
4899	,,	W. Holdsworth.	2944	,,	G. Lonsdale.
5734	,,	H. Venison.	3250	,,	T. Lown.
2739	Drummer	A. Coombs.*	1428	,,	J. Lupton.†
3115	Private	J. Ainsley.	5795	,,	J. Marchant.
2550	,,	E. Albany.	4173	,,	J. McGann.
2294	,,	W. Allen.*	3635	,,	J. Mee.
3110	,,	H. Baggaley.†*	3349	,,	W. Meehan.
4567	,,	J. Barker.	5940	,,	F. Moore.
3552	,,	P. Bartley.	2716	,,	J. Mullan.
5939	,,	J. Benson.*	6012	,,	W. Murray.
4593	,,	J. Best.	1619	,,	R. Nixon.†
4856	,,	F. Bingley.	2661	,,	G. Nolan.
5912	,,	W. Booth.	2709	,,	J. Parker.†
3372	,,	E. Brown.	5777	,,	H. Parker.
5960	,,	A. Bruce.*	2906	,,	H. Plenty.
5660	,,	J. Carson.	1346	,,	H. Powell.
2620	,,	T. Cave.	5718	,,	C. Raymond.
5741	,,	G. Challis.	5518	,,	L. Ricci.
2633	,,	F. Cole.	5897	,,	C. Riley.
888	,,	C. Coldwell.*	5448	,,	J. Robinson.
3140	,,	N. Cooling.	5798	,,	W. Rodgers.*
1157	,,	R. Donald.	4534	,,	E. Root.
3346	,,	J. Elliott.	2495	,,	W. Rose.
2702	,,	W. Fowler.	5506	,,	W. Rushworth.*
3171	,,	S. Francis.	5836	,,	J. Sharpe.
5827	Private	J. Simmonds.	1864	Private	J. Parker.
2457	,,	W. Skipsey.	2647	,,	J. Harrison.
2425	,,	J. Smith.	3598	,,	J. Lacy.
3741	,,	G. Spence.	2744	,,	J. Standley.†
2556	,,	H. Sutters.	5671	,,	C. Rawlings.
3214	,,	T. W. Swift.†	1957	,,	W. Bradbury.
2131	,,	T. Taylor.	4525	,,	H. Garside.†
2364	,,	J. Prest.	3132	,,	J. Burroughs.
5875	,,	S. Thompson.	3685	,,	M. Gargon.†

5875	,,	S. Thompson.	3685	,,	M. Gargon.†
5547	,,	J. Williams.	5376	,,	J. Wood.
5681	,,	T. Wimbleton.	5679	,,	H. Rolfe.
5554	,,	J. Windsor.	1533	,,	G. London.
5544	,,	J. Winzar.	3277	,,	D. Jones.
2535	,,	J. Woodman.			

MISSING AT PAARDEBERG, 18TH FEBRUARY, 1900.

4308 Private Barrett.†   5919 Private Poole.
3367 Private Bowler.

KILLED AT PAARDEBERG (KITCHENER'S KOP) 23RD FEBRUARY, 1900.

3549	Sergeant	B. Richardson.	5666	Private	K. Hardy.
2936	Private	J. Clarke.	5719	,,	J. Harwood.
3234	,,	J. Cram.	2304	,,	R. Raw.
3097	,,	A. Grigg.	4106	,,	G. Scruton.

2365 Private J. Wilkinson.

WOUNDED AT PAARDEBERG (KITCHENER'S KOP), 23RD FEBRUARY, 1900.

Captain G. Pearson (severely, legs).
Lieutenant M. E. T. Gunthorpe (slightly, arm).
2nd-Lieutenant E. V. L. Wardle (slightly, neck).

4038	Corporal	A. Dutfield.	2456	Private	E. Wilson.
5365	,,	W. Taylor.	5930	,,	T. Jackson.
3134	Private	C. Alton.	5911	,,	G. Jessop.
3552	,,	P. Bartley.	3227	,,	J. Holmes.
5076	,,	J. Bailey.	3909	,,	A. Hunter.
2844	,,	H. Buckle.	5670	,,	R. Ruddy,
1503	,,	J. Burke.	6013	,,	R. Rusted.
2532	,,	G. Burrows.	3895	,,	J. Christie†.
2708	,,	M. Gibson.	1285	,,	J. Williams.

KILLED AT DRIEFONTEIN, ORANGE FREE STATE, 10TH MARCH, 1900.

3252 Private G. Birks.

WOUNDED AT DRIEFONTEIN, 10TH MARCH, 1900.

3620	Sergeant	F. C. Hatton.	2616	Private	J. Lynch.†
3407	,,	H. Mackay.	3355	,,	J. Watson.
4121	Private	J. Bolton.*	3337	,,	J. Davis.
4992	,,	D Smith.*	2882	,,	F. C. Burgess.
5863	,,	J. Castle.	4062	,,	J. Lister.
4997	,,	W. Jones.	5348	,,	M. Hughes.
5685	,,	J. Rimmington.	3323	,,	E. Bennett.
5941	,,	J. Wootton.	2417	,,	J. Lockwood.
3879	,,	P. Carroll.†	6015	,,	G. Newton.
3279	,,	B. Keeley.	5392	,,	G. Woodhead.
2302	,,	F. Brown.	2869	,,	J. Clancy.

5993	,,	F. Townsend.	1182	,,	J. Duffy.
1532	,,	J. Bennett.	3586	,,	W. Wilson.†

WOUNDED IN ACTION AT SANNA'S POST, ORANGE FREE STATE, 31ST MARCH, 1900.

5632 Lance-Corporal A. Carter (4th M.I.).
2336 Private E. Holland (4th M.I.).   4571 Private J. Gamble (4th M.I.)

KILLED IN ACTION NEAR THABA N'CHU, ORANGE FREE STATE, 27TH APRIL, 1900.

2393 Private G. Humphries (2nd M.I.).

WOUNDED IN ACTION AT KAREE KLOOF, ORANGE FREE STATE, 30TH APRIL, 1900.

3291 Private E. Simpson (4th M.I.).

WOUNDED IN ACTION AT PRETORIA, 4TH JUNE, 1900.

6027 Private T. Hicken.

KILLED IN ACTION AT BALMORAL, TRANSVAAL, 12TH AUGUST, 1900.

2669 Private W. H. Varlow (4th M.I.).

WOUNDED IN ACTION AT BELFAST, TRANSVAAL, 24TH AUGUST, 1900.

Lieutenant W. G. Tarbet (slightly, wrist).
3305 Private W. Hawkins (4th M.I.).   2421 Private P. Broker (4th M.I.).
5547　,,　F. Axup　　,,　　4866　,,　W. Keighley　,,
5549 J. Ryan (4th M.I.), on 26th August.

WOUNDED IN ACTION, VILJOEN'S DRIFT, ORANGE RIVER COLONY, 6TH NOVEMBER, 1900.

3953 Private J. Daley (2nd M.I.).

WOUNDED IN ACTION, KLIPPLAAT'S DRIFT, TRANSVAAL, 16TH JULY, 1901.

5728 Private C. F. White (4th M.I.).

WOUNDED IN ACTION AT HOLFONTEIN, O.R.C., 29TH JULY, 1901.

6308 Private D. Hawthorne* (21st M.I.).

WOUNDED IN ACTION, HONING'S KLOOF, TRANSVAAL, 30TH JULY, 1901.

4465 Private F. Hainstock (4th M.I.)
5435　,,　H. Dearman　　,,

WOUNDED IN ACTION AT KRUGER'S POST, TRANSVAAL, 3RD OCTOBER, 1901.

4394 Drummer J. Tiller (4th M.I.).
2886 Private R. Winkle (4th M.I.).   5513 Private J. Green (4th M.I.).

WOUNDED IN ACTION IN THE ORIGSTAD VALLEY, TRANSVAAL,
4TH OCTOBER, 1901.

Lieutenant M. R. Liddon (4th M.I.), severely, thigh.

WOUNDED IN ACTION AT JORDAN SIDING, ORANGE RIVER COLONY,
14TH DECEMBER, 1901.

922 Sergeant-Instructor-Musketry W. Moy, P.S. 3rd Batt.

WOUNDED NEAR SPRINGS, TRANSVAAL, 25TH APRIL, 1902.

3618 Private J. Wardle.

WOUNDED IN ACTION AT PAARDEPLAATS, TRANSVAAL, 10TH MAY, 1902.

4155 Private J Greenwood (4th M.I.).

All men marked with an (*) died of Wounds. Those marked with a (†) were Militia Reservists of the 3rd or 4th Battalions.

DIED FROM VARIOUS CAUSES DURING THE CAMPAIGN.

Men marked with an (*) were attached for duty to the 3rd Battalion. The men marked with a (†) belong to the 3rd or 4th Battalions and were attached to the 1st.

208	Col.-Sergt.	H. Battye.*	6015	Private	J. Newton.
3613	,,	G. Stephenson.*	6016	,,	J. Nixon.
2697	Band-Sgt.	W. Hall.	7273	,,	E. Outhwaite (Vol.)
3347	Corporal	J. Nagginton.	4475	,,	J. Pinnock.
7324	,,	A. Stephenson (Vol.)	2439	,,	H. Portbury.
2991	,,	J. Bailey.	1722	,,	T. Burton.†
2898	,,	G. Collings.	3020	,,	J. Cavanagh.
1303	,,	D. Duffy.	2592	,,	G. Carlile.
6089	,,	D. Smithers.*	3432	,,	J. Conroy.
5928	Lc.-Cpl.	W. Stead.	5465	,,	J. Cameron.
5486	,,	H. Hobson.	2896	,,	J. Carpenter.
3644	,,	J. McCardle.	5961	,,	P. Carroll.
2565	,,	R. Stanton.	170	,,	J. Dibble.*
2848	,,	R. Johnson.	4367	,,	A. Woollett.
6096	,,	J. McHale.*	5679	,,	R. Rolfe.
6022	Drummer	H. Haines.*	2607	,,	F. Rouse.
3708	Private	J. Ackroyd.†	2495	,,	W. Rose.
2892	,,	G. Appleton.	5827	,,	W. Simmons.
3923	,,	H. Adamson.†	4484	,,	J. Smith.
4443	,,	J. Butterworth.†	1664	,,	J. Stephenson.
4590	,,	W. Baines.	5688	,,	G. Sullivan.
3540	,,	C. Bryant.	5854	,,	A. Sollars.*
2400	,,	O. Birmingham.	2533	,,	W. Sykes.
3978	,,	A. Benson.	3972	,,	W. Tighe.
6502	,,	H. Brummage.	6215	,,	J. Trickett.*
2715	,,	T. Dunn. ‡	6028	,,	C. Turton.
4052	,,	J. Dunford.†	2614	,,	A. Smith.†
1696	,,	J. Dixon.	3820	,,	G. Wilson.

7238	,,	J. Frost (Vol. Co.)	5936	,,	A. Wilkinson.
5977	,,	H. Fitton.	5569	,,	G. Webster.
2545	,,	A. Gosling.	5749	,,	H. White.
2945	,,	R. Goodwill.	6169	,,	R. Walker.*
1442	,,	A. Giles.	5535	,,	J. Pullan.
2676	,,	W. Gibbon.	2110	,,	E. Perkins.†
5701	,,	J. Gains.	3198	,,	J. Purvis.
3053	Private	J. Hagen.	6143	Private	J. Pease.*
3387	,,	F. Horton.	1044	,,	J. Pattison.
3038	,,	A. Dawson.	6244	,,	G. Pye.*
2784	,,	J. Kenney.	7553	,,	M. Dunn* (Vol. Co.)
2999	,,	H. Lane.	6233	,,	P. Foley.*
4854	,,	G. Lofthouse.	7257	,,	J. Stubbs (Vol. Co.)
5763	,,	R. Leeming.	6367	,,	H. Webb.
1653	,,	H. Marrow.	6248	,,	E. G. Worne.*
7319	,,	J. Milner. (Vol.)	5840	,,	J. Swales.‡
5236	,,	C. Matthews.			

‡Missing, presumed to be dead.

5806	Corporal	J. Buxton, died on passage home from South Africa.				
3626	,,	A. Tribe	,,	,,	,,	,, ,,
7322	Private	Sewell	,,	,,	to South Africa (Vol. Co.)	

APPENDIX C.

THE BATTLE OF DRIEFONTEIN.

Referring to this battle, the following passage occurs in "A Subaltern's Letters to his Wife":—

"Driefontein will long be remembered by the Essex, the Welsh and the Yorkshire regiments. They behaved splendidly, advancing to the attack against a steep series of kopjes in the teeth of a most destructive fire. The Essex did, perhaps, the best of all, for they passed through the other two regiments, taking ammunition from them when things were looking nasty."

The following letters, contradicting the latter part of this statement, are now published:—

From Lieut.-Col. C. WOOD, C.B., to Lieut.-Col. H. BOWLES, C.B.

PLATRAND, TRANSVAAL,
November 14th, 1901.

MY DEAR BOWLES,
    Re the battle of Driefontein you wrote me about. Your regiment (the Yorkshire) was on our (Essex) right the whole day at Driefontein, therefore the statement in R. Rankin's book ("A Subaltern's Letters to his Wife, p. 211), that we (Essex) passed through you, &c., is absolutely untrue. I can quite understand you wishing to have this statement rectified, and you are at liberty to make any use you like of this letter. Hoping you and the old regiment are going well and strong at Elandsfontein,

Believe me to be, yours sincerely,
CYRIL WOOD.

ASHMEAD, DURSLEY,
December 14th, 1901.

SIR,
    I beg to acknowledge the receipt of your letter with enclosure from Lieut.-Colonel Wood, Commanding 1st Essex Regiment. From

the evidence you have given me and from replies to enquiries instituted since your first letter, I am satisfied that the statement made in my book "A Subaltern's Letters to his Wife," p. 211, to the effect that the Essex Regiment passed through the Yorkshire Regiment, taking ammunition from the Yorkshires is incorrect, and I desire to express my regret that this statement, which shall be withdrawn in the next edition of the book, should have caused annoyance to yourself and the Yorkshire Regiment.

        I am, Sir,
         Yours truly,
           REGINALD RANKIN.

Lieut.-Colonel H. BOWLES, C.B.

APPENDIX D.

Army Orders—South Africa.

Bloemfontein, 14th March, 1900.

It affords the Field-Marshal Commanding-in-Chief the greatest pleasure in congratulating the Army in South Africa on the various events that have occurred during the past few weeks, and he would specially offer his sincere thanks to that portion of the Army which, under his immediate command, have taken part in the operations resulting yesterday in the capture of Bloemfontein.

On the 12th February this force crossed the boundary which divides the Orange Free State from British territory. Three days later Kimberley was relieved. On the 15th day the bulk of the Boer Army in this State, under one of their most trusted generals, were made prisoners. On the 17th day the news of the relief of Ladysmith was received, and on the 13th March, 29 days from the commencement of the operations, the capital of the Orange Free State was occupied.

This is a record of which any army may well be proud—a record which could not have been achieved except by earnest, well disciplined men, determined to do their duty and to surmount whatever difficulties or dangers might be encountered.

Exposed to extreme heat by day, bivouacking under heavy rain, marching long distances (not infrequently with reduced rations), the endurance, cheerfulness and gallantry displayed by all ranks are beyond praise, and Lord Roberts feels sure that neither Her Majesty the Queen nor the British nation will be unmindful of the efforts made by this force to uphold the honour of their country.

The Field-Marshal desires especially to refer to the fortitude and heroic spirit with which the wounded have borne their sufferings. Owing to the great extent of country over which modern battles have to be fought, it is not always possible to afford immediate aid to those who are struck down; many hours have indeed, at times, elapsed before some of the wounded could be attended to, but not a word of murmur or complaint has been uttered; the anxiety of all, when succour came, was that their comrades should be cared for first.

In assuring every officer and man how much he appreciates their efforts in the past, Lord Roberts is confident that in the future they will continue to show the same resolution and soldierly qualities, and to lay down their lives if need be (as so many brave men have already done) in order to ensure that the war in South Africa may be brought to a satisfactory conclusion.

By order,

W. F. KELLY, Major-General,
Deputy-Adjutant-General for Chief of the Staff.

Pretoria, 7th June, 1900.

In congratulating the British Army in South Africa on the occupation of Johannesburg and Pretoria, the one being the principal town and the other the capital of the Transvaal, and also on the relief of Mafeking, after an heroic defence of over 200 days, the Field-Marshal, Commanding-in-Chief, desires to place on record his high appreciation of the gallantry and endurance displayed by the troops, both those who have taken part in the advance across the Vaal river, and those who have been employed in the less arduous duty of protecting the line of communication through the Orange River Colony. After the force reached Bloemfontein on the 13th March, it was necessary to halt there for a certain period, as railway communication with Cape Colony had to be restored before supplies and necessaries of all kinds could be got up from the base. The rapid advance from the Modder river and the want of forage *en route*, had told hardly on the horses of the cavalry and artillery, and the transport mules and oxen, and to replace these casualties, a considerable number of animals had to be provided. Throughout the six weeks the army remained halted at Bloemfontein, the enemy showed considerable activity, especially in the south-eastern portion of the Orange River Colony, but by the beginning of May everything was in readiness for a further advance into the enemy's country, and on the 2nd of that month active operations were again commenced.

On the 12th of May, Kroonstadt, where Mr. Steyn had established the so-called Government of the Orange Free State, was entered, and on the 17th of May, Mafeking was relieved. On the 31st of May, Johannesburg was occupied, and on the 5th of June, the British flag waved over Pretoria.

During these 35 days the main body of the force marched 300 miles, including fifteen days' halt, and engaged the enemy on six different occasions. The column under Lieut.-General Ian Hamilton marched 400 miles in forty-five days, including ten days' halt. It was engaged with the enemy twenty-eight times. The flying column under the command of Colonel B. Mahon, which relieved Mafeking, marched at the rate of nearly fifteen miles a day for fourteen consecutive days, and successfully accomplished its object, despite the determined opposition offered by the enemy.

During the recent operations, the sudden variations in temperature between the warm sun in the daytime and the bitter cold at night, have been peculiarly trying to the troops, and owing to the necessity for rapid movement, the soldiers have frequently had to bivouac, after long and trying marches, without firewood, and on scanty rations. The cheerful spirit with which difficulties have been overcome and hardships disregarded, are deserving of the highest praise, and in thanking all ranks for their successful efforts to obtain the objects in view, Lord Roberts is proud to think that the soldiers under his command have worthily upheld the traditions of Her Majesty's Army in fighting, in marching, and in the admirable discipline which has been maintained throughout a period of extraordinary trial and difficulty.

Farewell Order to the 11th Division by Lieut.-General Pole-Carew.

In bidding farewell to the troops lately forming the 11th Division, General Pole-Carew begs to thank all ranks from the bottom of his heart for the admirable manner in which they have invariably carried out the duties trusted to them. He congratulates them sincerely on the cheerful and soldierlike spirit with which they have borne the hardships of the campaign, and he ventures to think they have made a name for the division which is second to none in South Africa.

He wishes them all the best of fortune in the future. He feels certain when opportunity may offer they will certainly add to the laurels they have so well earned, and he only hopes that some day he may again have the great privilege of association with them.

General Pole-Carew trusts that officers, non-commissioned officers and men will understand how deeply gratified he is for all the good work they have done, and how sincerely he regrets to be obliged to say, now, "Good-bye."

By order,
L. Hamilton, Colonel, A.A.G.

Komati Poort,
October, 1900.

Farewell Order by Lord Kitchener.

Army Headquarters, South Africa,
June 23rd, 1902.

Before leaving South Africa, the General Officer Commanding-in-Chief wishes to express his best thanks to all general officers, officers, non-commissioned officers and men for the excellent service they have rendered since he first took over command, some eighteen months ago. The period in question has offered few opportunities for those decisive engagements which keep up the spirit of an army, and add brilliance and interest to its operations. On the other hand, officers and men have been called upon for unceasing and ever increasing exertions, in face of great hardships and difficulties, against a dangerous and elusive antagonist. The conduct of the troops under these trying circumstances has been beyond all praise. Never has there been the smallest sign of slackness or impatience; and it seems to Lord Kitchener that the qualities of endurance and resolution thus displayed are much more valuable to a Commander than any dashing or short-lived effort by which some hard-fought actions may be won in a campaign of ordinary duration.

The General Officer Commanding-in-Chief has also special pleasure in congratulating the Army on the kindly and humane spirit by which all ranks have been animated during this long struggle. Fortunately for the future of South Africa the truth in this matter is known to our late enemy as well as to ourselves, and no misrepresentations from outside can prevail in the long-run against the actual fact that no war has ever yet been waged in which combatants and non-combatants, on either side, have shown so much consideration and kindness to one another.

This message would be incomplete if reference were not made to the soldierly qualities displayed throughout the campaign by our quondam enemies, and to the admirable spirit displayed by them in carrying out the surrender of their arms.

Many of the Boer leaders, who at an earlier date recognised the futility of carrying on a devastating conflict beyond a certain point, have already for some time, served with us in the field, and the help which they rendered us will not be forgotten. Many also of those who continued the struggle to the end have expressed a hope that on some future occasion they may have an opportunity of serving side by side with His Majesty's Forces, from whom Lord Kitchener can assure them they will receive a very hearty welcome.

In bidding the Army of South Africa farewell, it only remains for Lord Kitchener to wish every individual serving therein all happiness and prosperity for the future.

REGIMENTAL ORDER ON THE DEPARTURE OF THE FIRST VOLUNTEER CONTINGENT.

Nelspruit, 10th October, 1900.

The Commanding Officer cannot allow Captain Bell, the officers and n.c.o.'s and men of the Volunteer company to leave his command without expressing his approval of the work they have performed since they joined the battalion at Springfield, outside Bloemfontein, in April last.

They one and all picked up their duties quickly, and performed them entirely to his satisfaction.

On the occasion when the company was under fire, crossing the Vet river, and also outside Pretoria, they displayed great coolness, and the Commanding Officer only hopes that should the regiment be again called upon to go on service in any part of the world, one or more of the Volunteer companies will offer their services, and take the rough with the smooth, as the Volunteer company to which he bids farewell to-day have done.

By order,
GERARD CHRISTIAN,
Captain and Adjutant.

Farewell Letter from Major-Gen. Stephenson, C.B.

Extract from Regimental Orders.

Pretoria, 22nd August, 1901.

No. 4.—The following letter, received from Major-Gen. Stephenson, C.B., is published for information:—

"General Stephenson cannot allow the 1st Battalion, The Princess of Wales's Own Yorkshire Regiment to leave his command without expressing his very hearty appreciation of their splendid services throughout the campaign. The 1st Yorkshire Regiment joined the 18th Brigade on its formation at Modder river, on the 6th February, 1900, and from the first showed fine endurance and the highest soldierly qualities.

"Whether on the march, in action, or on outpost duty, General Stephenson has always had the most perfect confidence in this grand old regiment, and he has never been disappointed. He knows well from long experience that any service that the 1st Yorkshire may have the honour of rendering for the British Empire in the future, will be nobly and gallantly performed. It is with the keenest personal regret that General Stephenson now has to bid good-bye to his well-tried comrades of the last battalion to leave his command of the old 18th Brigade.

"May the highest honour and success attend them, one and all, wherever they go.

"T. E. Stephenson, Major-General,

"Commanding 18th Brigade."

APPENDIX E.

THE YORKSHIRE SECTION NORTHERN COMPANY, 2nd BATT. MOUNTED INFANTRY.

ON MOBILIZATION AT ALDERSHOT, OCTOBER, 1899.

Lieutenant M. H. Tomlin.

4159	Col.-Sergt.	Cushen, W.	2904	Private	Healey, W.
4157	Sergeant	Wilson, H.	5327	,,	Hodge, W.
3948	Lc.-Corpl.	Hewitt, L.	2393	,,	Humphries, G.
5117	,,	Paton, J.	5804	,,	Jerritt, F.
3644	Drummer	McCardle, J.	3155	,,	Long, E.
5848	Private	Akers, R.	3208	,,	Lyne, M.
4897	,,	Andrews, E.	3099	,,	Miller, A.
4279	,,	Armstrong, H.	2960	,,	Milling, R.
2779	,,	Close, W.	4914	,,	Morgan, I.
2441	,,	Crosby, J.	4957	,,	Parkinson, J.
3953	,,	Daley, J.	3945	,,	Seymour, G.
4970	,,	Davis, I.	4166	,,	Taylor, A.
4700	,,	Dawe, T.	4968	,,	Whitehurst, H.
4595	,,	Fallowell, S.	4573	,,	Willis, S.
5285	,,	Gardner, J.	4766	,,	Worton, S.
4918	,,	Garry, J.	4923	,,	Wright, H.
5366	,,	Gowlett, W.	3015	,,	Yates, J.
3025	,,	Hamilton, W.			

2ND M.I. CASUALTIES.

	Killed	Wounded	Died of Wounds.
Officers	5	11	—
N.C.O's. and Men ..	30	105	10
Total	35	116	10

RECORD OF BOERS KILLED, CAPTURED, &C., BY 2ND M.I.

Boers killed, 6; wounded, 13; prisoners, 310; armed natives, 6; wagons, 43; carts, 57; guns, 7; rifles, 234; horses, 622; oxen, 8,531; sheep, 74,931; helios, 4; S.A.A., 4,662.

APPENDIX F.

MENTIONED IN DESPATCHES.

Lieut.-General Lord Methuen's Report.

BELMONT, *Nov.* 20*th*, 1899.

Captain Bulfin, Brigade-Major, on whose shoulders great responsibility rested, did admirable work.

From Lieut.-Colonel Money's Report.

ENSLIN, *Nov.* 25*th*, 1899.

Captain Bulfin rendered me great assistance, and was near me at the final assault.

From Lord Methuen's Despatch.

MODDER RIVER, *Dec.* 1*st*, 1899.

Captain Bulfin, Yorkshire Regiment, did his duty admirably.

From Lieut-General French's Despatch.

February 2*nd*, 1900.

Colesberg, Dec. 15th, 1899 to January 25th, 1900.

Lieut.-Colonel H. Bowles has done very good service at critical times in command of his battalion.

Captain M. H. Orr was dangerously wounded during the attack on New Zealand Hill, which post he commanded with great credit.

Lord Roberts in his Despatch of March 31*st*, 1900, *brings to notice the following:—*

Lieut.-Colonel H. Bowles.   Captain M. L. Ferrar.
Major J. A. Fearon.   3549 Sergeant B. Richardson
5684 Lance-Corporal A. Hatton.

In Lord Roberts' Despatch ending with the occupation of Komati Poort in September, 1900, but which was not dated till September 4th, 1901, the following Officers, Non-Commissioned Officers and Men are mentioned for Special and Meritorious Services:—

1ST BATTALION.
OFFICERS.

Captain M. L. Ferrar.   Lieutenant C. F. C. Jarvis.
  ,,   G. Pearson.   ,,   E. V. L. Wardle.
  ,,   E. M. Esson.   2nd-Lieut. A. C. Neave (deceased).
  ,,   G. Christian.   Qr.-Mr. and Hon. Capt. C. Organ.
Lieutenant C. V. Edwards.

WARRANT OFFICER, NON-COMMISSIONED OFFICERS AND MEN.

Sergt.-Major A. J. Hughes.   5684 Corporal A. Hatton.
2367 Col.-Sergeant J. Walker.   2675 Lnce.-Corporal A. Philpot.
1910   ,,   W. Bryant.   2701 Private F. Eyre.
3472   ,,   E. Pickard.   4300   ,,   W. Burns.
3961   ,,   B. Williams.   3243   ,,   J. Hayes.
3407 Sergeant H. S. Mackay.   3183   ,,   W. Hewitt.
3549   ,,   B. Richardson.   1142   ,,   W. Usher.
2898 Corporal G. F. Collings.   1106   ,,   W. Pearson.
1285 Private J. Williams.

MOUNTED INFANTRY.
OFFICERS.

Captain H. G. Holmes.   Lieutenant W. G. Tarbet.
Lieutenant T. W. Stansfeld.   ,,   M. M. H. Nevile.

NON-COMMISSIONED OFFICERS AND MEN.

4159 Col.-Sergeant W. Cushen.   2715 Private T. Dunn.
4159 Sergeant H. Wilson.   5227   ,,   F. Wright.
2397   ,,   A. Couldrey.   2987   ,,   F. Bushby.
3098 Lnce.-Corpl. J. M. Hyland.   5327   ,,   W. H. Hodge.
2764   ,,   G. T. Atkinson.   2795   ,,   H. Edmonds.
7307   ,,   H. Beecroft (Vol.).   4710   ,,   T. W. Schofield.

ATTACHED TO MILITIA BATTALIONS.
OFFICERS.

Captain C. A. C. King.   Captain A. F. Owen Lewis.
Quarter-Master and Hon. Captain G. Croft.

WARRANT OFFICER AND NON-COMMISSIONED OFFICERS.

Sergeant-Major G. J. Smith.   Colour-Sergeant P. Hall.
Qr.-Mr.-Sergeant J. Lowther.   Sergeant S. Rushton.

Lord Kitchener's Mentions—

July 28th, 1901.

Captain M. H. Tomlin (M.I.) in a most daring manner rode with twenty men through a deep kloof to head of convoy, and under heavy fire stopped it.

August 8th, 1901.

Lieutenant M. M. H. Nevile (M.I.) for skill and enterprise in surprising laager in Bothas-berg, July 13th, when he captured eight Boers and a considerable number of stock and wagons.

December 8th, 1901.

Captain (Local Major) H. G. Holmes for good service in command of detached bodies of troops in Kroonstad district.

Lieutenant W. B. Walker (M.I.) in command of a section retiring before superior force at Kaffir Spruit, October 5th, a sergeant's horse being killed, he returned under fire and helped him along to safety.

Lord Roberts' Final Recommendations—

March 1st, 1902.

2520 Private E. Carss (M.I.).

Lord Kitchener's Final Despatch—

June 23rd, 1902.

OFFICERS.

Major M. H. Orr.   Lieutenant M. E. T. Gunthorpe.

WARRANT OFFICER, NON-COMMISSIONED OFFICER AND MEN.

Sergeant-Major J. Walker.   Colour-Sergeant H. Parkinson (M.I.)
4300 Private W. Burns.   5327 Private W. H. Hodge (M.I.)

OFFICER AND NON-COMMISSIONED OFFICERS ATTACHED TO THE MILITIA.

Captain and Adjutant C. A. C. King.

NON-COMMISSIONED OFFICERS.

Qr.-Mr.-Sergeant J. Lowther.   Sergt-Inst. of Musketry W. Moy.

HONOURS AND PROMOTIONS.

THE VICTORIA CROSS.

It was announced in the "Gazette," of August 8th, 1902, that the King had been graciously pleased to approve of the decoration of the Victoria Cross being delivered to the representatives of the under-mentioned non-commissioned officer who fell during the recent operations in South Africa in the performance of an act of valour, which would, in the opinion of the Commander-in-Chief of the Forces in the Field, have entitled him to be recommended for that distinction had he survived.

Sergeant A. Atkinson, Yorkshire Regiment.

During the Battle of Paardeberg, February 18th, 1900, Sergeant A. A. Atkinson, 1st Battalion Yorkshire Regiment went out seven times under heavy and close fire to obtain water for the wounded. At the seventh attempt he was wounded in the head, and died a few days afterwards.

To be Companion of the Order of the Bath.
Lieutenant-Colonel H. Bowles.

To be Companions of the Distinguished Service Order.

Major M. H. Orr.   Captain G. Christian.
Captain A. F. Owen Lewis.   Lieutenant T. W. Stansfeld.
Lieutenant E. V. Livesey Wardle.   Lieutenant W. G. Tarbet.

Brevet Rank.

To be Brevet-Lieut.-Col. Major J. A. Fearon   .. 29th Nov., 1900.
            ,,   Major   Captain M. L. Ferrar .. 29th Nov., 1900.
            ,,   ,,   ,,   E. S. Bulfin .. 29th Nov., 1900.
            ,,   ,,   ,,   H. G. Holmes.. 26th June, 1902.
            ,,   ,,   ,,   M. H. Tomlin.. 26th June, 1902.
            ,,   ,,   ,,   C. A. C. King.. 22nd Aug., 1902.
            ,,   Lieut.-Col. Major   E. S. Bulfin .. 26th June, 1902.

To have the Honorary Rank of Major.
Quarter-Master and Honorary Captain C. Organ.

Awarded the Distinguished Conduct Medal.

Sergeant-Major J. Walker.   Colour-Sergeant E. Pickard.
Colour-Sergeant B. Williams.   Colr.-Sergeant H. Parkinson (M.I.)
Sergeant A. Couldrey (M.I.).   Sergeant H. Wilson (M.I.).
Corporal G. F. Collings.   Lnce-Corpl. J. M. Hyland (M.I.).
Lnce.-Corpl. H. Beecroft (Vol. M.I.) Private H. Edmonds (M.I.).
Lnce.-Corporal W. Philpot.   Lnce.-Corpl. G. T. Atkinson (M.I.).
Private J. Hayes.   Private W. Pearson.
Private W. Usher.   Private E. Carss (M.I.).
                    Private F. Eyre.

Attached to Militia (3rd Battalion).
Sergeant-Major G. J. Smith.   Qr.-Mr.-Sergeant J. Lowther.

APPENDIX G.

Roll of Officers who Served with the 1st Battalion during the War.

Rank and Name.	Relief of Kimberley	Paardeberg	Driefontein	Johannesburg	Diamond Hill	Belfast	Cape Colony	Orange Free State	Transvaal	South Africa, 1901.	South Africa, 1902.	King's Medal.	Remarks.
Lieut.-Colonel H. Bowles, C.B.	x	x	—	x	x	x	—	—	—	—	—	x	In command of Battalion during the War. Twice mentioned in Despatches. Severely wounded at Paardeberg. Awarded the C.B.
Major and Bt.-Lieut.-Col. J. A. Fearon.	x	x	x	x	x	x	—	—	—	—	—	x	Commandant Wynberg. In command of Depôt Battalion. Mentioned in Despatches. Brevet of Lieut.-Colonel.
Major G. C. S. Handcock	—	x	—	x	x	x	—	—	—	—	—	x	In command of 4th M.I., afterwards in command of M.I. Depôt.
Major T. D. Kirkpatrick	x	x	—	—	—	—	—	—	—	—	—	—	Severely wounded at Paardeberg. Invalided.
Major J. T. Cotesworth	—	—	—	—	—	x	x	x	—	—	—	—	Joined at Edendale. Commandant Kaapmuiden.
Major M. H. Orr, D.S.O.	—	—	x	x	—	x	x	x	—	—	—	x	Severely wounded at Slingersfontein, Cape Colony. Awarded the D.S.O. Twice mentioned in Despatches.
Captain and Bt.-Major M. L. Ferrar.	x	x	x	x	x	x	—	—	—	—	—	x	Commandant Springs. In command of Depôt Battalion. Twice mentioned in Despatches. Brevet of Major.

Name												Remarks
Captain G. Pearson	—	x	x	x	x	—	—	—	—	x		Severely wounded at Kitchener's Kop. Mentioned in Despatches.
Captain E. M. Esson	—	—	—	—	—	—	x	—	—	—		Mentioned in Despatches. Station Staff Officer Komati Poort.
Captain E. Somervell	—	—	—	—	—	—	x	—	—	—		Assistant Railway Transport Officer, Cape-town.
Captain and Bt.-Major H. G. Holmes	—	—	x	—	—	—	x	—	—	—		Joined at Bloemfontein. Served with 4th M.I. In command of 15th M.I., also a Mobile Column. Twice mentioned in Despatches. Brevet of Major.
Captain B. C. W. Williams	—	—	x	x	—	—	x	—	—	—		
Captain G. Christian, D.S.O.	—	—	x	x	—	—	x	x	—	—		Adjutant, 16th December, 1899, to 29th November, 1900. Served as Staff Officer, Town Guards, Cape Town. Mentioned in Despatches. Awarded the D.S.O.
Captain H. F. Lea	—	x	—	x	x	x	—	x	—	x	x	Joined at Komati Poort. Station Staff Officer, Elandsfontein. Afterwards on Staff as Assistant Provost-Marshal. Placed on list of officers considered qualified for Staff employment.
Captain M. R. Liddon	—	x	—	x	x	—	—	x	—	x	x	Joined at Springfield Kop. Served with 4th M.I. Severely wounded in Origstadt Valley, Transvaal.
Lieutenant C. V. Edwards	—	x	—	x	x	—	—	x	—	x	x	Joined at Rensberg. Severely wounded at Paardeberg. Mentioned in Despatches.
Lieutenant C. F. C. Jarvis	—	x	—	—	x	x	—	—	—	—	—	Invalided. Mentioned in Despatches.
Lieutenant M. E. T. Gunthorpe	x	x	—	—	x	x	—	—	x	x	x	Joined at De Aar. Was present at Stormberg with Royal Irish Rifles. Served as Transport Officer and Adjutant to Battalion. Slightly wounded at Kitchener's Kop. Mentioned in Despatches.

APPENDIX G.—ROLL OF OFFICERS WHO SERVED WITH THE 1st BATTALION DURING THE WAR.

Rank and Name.	Queen's Medal and Clasps.										King's Medal.	Remarks.
	Relief of Kimberley.	Paardeberg.	Driefontein.	Johannesburg.	Diamond Hill.	Belfast.	Cape Colony.	Orange Free State.	Transvaal.	South Africa, 1901.	South Africa, 1902.	
Lieutenant W. B. Walker	—	—	—	—	x	x	x	x	—	—	—	x	Joined at Bloemfontein. Served with 2nd M.I. Mentioned in Despatches.
Lieutenant R. H. Darwin	x	x	x	x	x	x	—	—	—	—	—	x	Regimental Transport Officer. Employed with Army Service Corps. Staff Officer for Prisoners of War.
Lieut. E. V. L. Wardle, D.S.O.	x	x	—	x	x	x	—	—	—	—	—	x	Slightly wounded at Kitchener's Kop. Awarded the D.S.O.
Lieut. T. W. Stansfeld, D.S.O.	x	x	x	x	x	x	—	—	—	—	—	x	Acted as A.D.C. to Br.-General Stephenson. Served with 4th M.I. Mentioned in Despatches. Awarded the D.S.O., and promoted into the Royal Warwickshire Regiment.
Lieutenant W. G. Tarbet, D.S.O.	x	x	x	—	—	x	—	—	—	—	—	x	Served as Adjutant, 4th M.I. Slightly wounded at Klipdrift and Belfast. Mentioned in Despatches. Awarded the D.S.O.
Lieutenant M. M. H. Nevile.	x	x	x	x	x	x	—	—	—	—	—	x	Served with the 4th M.I. Twice Mentioned in Despatches. Specially promoted into the 5th Fusiliers.
Lieutenant C. H. de St. P. Bunbury.	x	x	x	x	x	x	—	—	—	—	—	x	Employed with Army Service Corps.
Lieutenant E. S. Broun	x	x	x	x	x	x	—	—	—	—	—	x	

Name													Notes
2nd-Lieut. A. C. Neave	–	x	–	–	–	–	–	–	–	–	–	–	Joined at De Aar. Mentioned in Despatches. Killed at Paardeberg.
Lieutenant H. V. Bastow	x	–	–	–	x	x	x	–	–	–	–	–	Joined at Bloemfontein. Employed with Remount Depôt. Afterwards in command of Convalescent Depôt, Germiston. Served with 4th M.I.
Lieutenant J. C. Morgan	x	–	–	–	x	x	x	x	–	–	–	–	Joined at Brandfort. Railway Staff Officer, Neispruit. Garrison Adjutant, Barberton. Served with 4th M.I.
Lieut. F. G. O. Sanderson	–	–	–	–	x	x	x	x	–	–	–	–	Joined at Pretoria. Invalided.
Lieutenant C. H. Marsden	–	x	x	–	x	x	x	x	–	–	x	–	Joined at Barberton.
Lieutenant H. W. McCall	–	x	x	x	x	x	x	x	–	–	–	–	Joined at Barberton.
Lieut. E. G. C. Bagshawe	–	–	x	x	x	x	x	–	–	–	–	–	Joined at Wonderfontein.
Lieut. B. H. Leatham ...	–	x	x	–	–	x	–	–	x	–	–	–	Joined at Barberton. Served with 4th M.I.
2nd-Lieut. B. C. D. Nash-Wortham.	–	x	x	–	–	–	–	–	–	–	–	–	Joined at Barberton, from 3rd Battalion. Station Staff Officer, Elandsfontein.
2nd-Lieut. L. D. Massy	–	x	–	–	–	–	–	–	–	–	x	–	Joined at Barberton. To Indian Army.
2nd-Lieut. R. F. Howard	–	x	–	–	–	–	–	–	–	–	–	–	Joined at Elandsfontein.
2nd-Lieut. C. G. Jeffery	–	–	–	–	–	–	–	–	–	–	–	–	Promoted from ranks or Special Service Company. To 2nd Battalion.
2nd-Lieut. B. L. Maddison	x	–	–	–	–	–	–	–	–	–	–	–	Joined at Elandsfonteir.
2nd-Lieut. S. L. Whatford	–	–	–	–	–	–	–	–	–	–	–	–	Joined at Elandsfontein, from 4th Battalion. Served with M.I.

APPENDIX G.—ROLL OF OFFICERS WHO SERVED WITH THE 1st BATTALION DURING THE WAR.

Rank and Name.	Queen's Medal and Clasps.											King's Medal.	Remarks.
	Relief of Kimberley	Paardeberg	Driefontein	Johannesburg	Diamond Hill	Belfast	Cape Colony	Orange Free State	Transvaal	South Africa, 1901.	South Africa, 1902.		
2nd-Lieut. J. H. S. Westley	—	—	—	—	—	—	x	x	x	—	x	—	Joined at Elandsfontein.
2nd-Lieut. C. E. Moss-Blundell.	—	—	—	—	—	—	x	x	x	—	x	—	Joined at Elandsfontein.
2nd-Lieut. G. P. Stevens	—	—	—	—	—	—	x	x	x	—	x	—	Joined at Elandsfontein.
2nd-Lieut. A. F. Bone ...	—	—	—	—	—	—	x	x	x	—	x	—	Joined at Elandsfontein. Served with Imperial Yeomanry and 4th Battalion.
Hon. Major and Qr.-Mr. C. Organ.	x	x	x	x	x	x	—	—	—	—	—	x	Quarter-Master to Battalion throughout the War. Mentioned in Despatches. Granted Hon. rank of Major.
Hon. Lieut. and Qr.-Mr. A. J. Hughes.	x	x	x	—	x	x	—	—	—	—	—	x	Served as Serjeant-Major, 1st Battalion. Promoted Qr.-Mr. 3rd Battalion. Mentioned in Despatches.

Officers Attached to the Battalion.

Rank and Name.	Relief of Kimberley	Paardeberg	Driefontein	Johannesburg	Diamond Hill	Belfast	Cape Colony	Orange Free State	Transvaal	South Africa, 1901	South Africa, 1902	King's Medal	Remarks.
Capt. H. R. S. Maitland (Reserve of Officers.)	—	—	—	—	—	—	1	1	—	—	—	1	Joined at Brandfort. Granted rank of Major in Reserve of Officers.
Captain M. H. L. Bell...	—	—	—	1	1	1	1	1	—	—	—	—	Joined at Springfield Kop with 1st Section Volunteer Service Company.
Lieutenant Houseman...	—	—	—	1	1	1	1	1	—	—	—	—	
Lieutenant Ewart	—	—	—	1	—	1	1	1	—	—	—	—	
Lieut. H. C. Matthews	1	—	—	—	—	—	1	1	1	1	—	—	Joined at Kaapmuiden with 2nd Section of the Volunteer Service Company, Officer Commanding Rest Camp, Elandsfontein.
Captain A. C. Buckle...	—	1	—	—	—	—	—	—	—	—	—	—	South Staffordshire Regiment, Joined at De Aar. Dangerously wounded at Paardeberg.
Lieutenant A. P. Strange	—	—	—	—	—	—	1	1	1	—	1	—	3rd Battalion Royal Berkshire Regiment. Joined at Elandsfontein.
2nd-Lieut. C. Newington	—	—	—	—	—	—	1	1	1	1	1	—	3rd Battalion Royal Lancaster Regiment. Joined at Elandsfontein.
Lieutenant W. A. S. de Gale.	—	—	—	—	—	—	1	1	1	—	1	—	3rd Battalion Northamptonshire Regiment. Joined at Elandsfontein.

APPENDIX G.

OFFICERS OF THE REGIMENT WHO SERVED IN SOUTH AFRICA DURING THE WAR NOT INCLUDED IN ABOVE ROLLS.

RANK AND NAME.	REMARKS.
Captain A. L. Napier	Brought a draft of 150 men from India to Elandsfontein, and returned with a similar number. Queen's Medal and two Clasps.
Captain and Brevet-Major C. A. C. King ...	Served with 3rd Battalion as Adjutant. Twice mentioned in Despatches. Brevet of Major. Queen's Medal with two Clasps, and King's Medal.
Captain D. L. Hartley	Served with 4th M.I. Queen's Medal and five Clasps.
Captain and Bt.-Lieut.-Col. E. S. Bulfin ...	On Staff. Engagements of Belmont, Enslin, Modder River, and Magersfontein. In command of a mobile column. Mentioned in Despatches. Brevets of Major and Lieutenant-Colonel. Queen's Medal with four Clasps, and King's Medal.
Captain and Brevet-Major M. H. Tomlin ...	Served with 2nd M.I., afterwards on Staff. In command of 9th M.I., and also a mobile column. Mentioned in Despatches. Brevet of Major. Queen's Medal with three Clasps, and King's Medal.
Captain H. E. Raymond	Assistant Provost-Marshal to 9th Division. Queen's Medal with three Clasps.
Captain A. F. Owen Lewis, D.S.O.	Served as Adjutant 6th Battalion, The Lancashire Fusiliers. District Commandant in Cape Colony. Mentioned in Despatches. Awarded the D.S.O. Queen's Medal with three Clasps.

Captain E. H. L. Warner	Employed with Railway Pioneer Regiment. Queen's Medal with three Clasps. King's Medal.
Lieutenant E. G. Caffin	Attached to Devonshire Regiment in Natal. Present at Elandslaagte, Rietfontein, Lombards Kop, and Defence of Ladysmith. Severely wounded. Queen's Medal with two Clasps. Promoted into 5th Fusiliers.
Lieutenant C. H. J. Noble	Employed as Transport Officer in Ladysmith. Promoted into the Manchester Regiment, and killed near Bethlehem, O.R.C., 12th November, 1901.
Lieutenant A. C. D. Pearson	At Capetown. Queen's Medal and two Clasps.
2nd-Lieutenant G. C. Denton	Served with 3rd Battalion. Queen's Medal and three Clasps. Appointed to 2nd Battalion.
2nd-Lieutenant J. H. C. Gardner	Promoted from 1st Royal Dragoons to 2nd Battalion. Queen's Medal and six Clasps.
2nd-Lieutenant H. J. Kirkpatrick	Transferred from Durham Light Infantry Militia to 2nd Battalion. Queen's Medal and Clasp.
Hon. Captain and Qr.-Mstr. G. Croft	Quarter-Master to 3rd Battalion. Queen's Medal and three Clasps.
Hon. Lieut. and Qr.-Mstr. J. Sheridan	Quarter-Master to 4th Battalion. Queen's Medal and two Clasps.

APPENDIX H.

Roll of Warrant and Non-commissioned Officers, shewing rank held at end of War.

Regimental Number	Rank and Name	Queen's Medal and Clasps.											King's Medal.	Remarks.
		Relief of Kimberley.	Paardeberg.	Driefontein.	Johannesburg.	Diamond Hill.	Belfast.	Cape Colony.	Orange Free State.	Transvaal.	South Africa, 1901.	South Africa, 1902.		
2819	Lce.-Sergt. J. Alderson	x	x	x	x	x	x	—	—	—	—	—	x	
3060	Corporal L. Armstrong	x	x	x	x	x	x	—	—	—	—	—	x	
5707	Corporal A. Armstrong	x	x	x	x	x	x	—	—	—	—	—	x	
3515	Col.-Sergt. F. Ashman...	x	x	—	—	x	x	—	—	—	—	—	—	
3264	Sergeant A. Atkinson ...	x	x	—	—	—	x	—	—	—	—	—	—	Died of wounds at Paardeberg. Awarded the V.C.
2991	Corporal J. Bailey	x	x	x	x	x	x	—	—	—	—	—	x	
4070	Sergeant A. J. Bailey ...	x	x	x	x	x	x	—	—	—	—	—	—	Drowned at Nelspruit.
3505	Sergeant F. Bannard ...	x	x	x	x	—	x	—	—	—	x	—	—	
6469	Corporal G. Baker	—	—	—	—	—	—	x	x	x	—	x	—	Served in 19th M.I.

		Served with 4th M.I.							Served with 4th M.I. Specially mentioned in Battalion Orders for good work.							Mentioned in Despatches.
2689	Corporal H. Barker ...	—	—	×	—	×	×	—	—	×	—	—	×	×	—	—	×
7290	Corporal F. Barr ...	—	—	—	×	—	—	—	—	—	—	×	—	—	—	×	—
4888	Sergeant F. Bell ...	—	—	—	—	—	—	—	—	—	×	—	—	×	×	—	—
4337	Corporal F. Benning ...	—	—	—	×	×	—	×	—	—	—	×	×	×	—	×	—
6058	Corporal F. Binns ...	—	×	×	×	×	—	—	—	—	—	—	—	—	—	—	—
3464	Corporal C. Birks ...	—	×	×	×	×	—	—	—	—	—	—	—	—	—	—	—
7335	Corporal E. J. Biggins ...	—	×	—	—	—	×	×	×	—	—	—	—	—	×	—	×
2825	Sergeant H. R. Blanche ...	—	×	×	—	—	×	×	×	—	—	—	—	—	×	—	×
4972	Corporal W. Blower ...	—	×	×	—	—	—	×	×	×	—	—	—	—	×	—	×
4066	Sergeant W. Boyle ...	—	—	—	—	×	—	×	×	—	—	×	×	×	×	—	×
4659	Corporal T. Bramley ...	×	—	—	—	—	×	—	×	×	—	×	×	×	×	—	×
5815	Corporal B. Braye ...	×	—	—	—	—	×	—	×	×	—	×	×	×	×	—	×
3093	Corporal W. Brown ...	×	—	—	—	×	—	×	×	—	×	×	×	×	—	×
2860	Corporal G. Brown ...	—	—	—	—	—	—	—	—	—	—	—	—	—	—	—
4396	Sergeant F. A. Brunton ...	—	—	—	—	—	—	—	—	—	—	—	—	—	—	—
1910	Q.-M. Sergt. W. Bryant	—	—	—	—	—	—	—	—	—	—	—	—	—	—	—

APPENDIX H.—ROLL OF WARRANT AND NON-COMMISSIONED OFFICERS, SHEWING RANK HELD AT END OF WAR.

Regimental Number	Rank and Name	Queen's Medal and Clasps											King's Medal	Remarks
		Relief of Kimberley	Paardeberg	Driefontein	Johannesburg	Diamond Hill	Belfast	Cape Colony	Orange Free State	Transvaal	South Africa, 1901.	South Africa, 1902.		
4092	Sergeant F. C. Burgess	x	x	x	x	x	x	—	—	—	—	—	x	
4683	Corporal H. Butcher ...	—	—	—	—	—	—	—	—	x	x	—	—	
5866	Corporal J. Buxton ...	x	x	x	x	x	x	—	—	—	—	—	x	Died on passage home. Served in 4th M.I.
4936	Sergeant E. Carter ...	x	x	x	x	x	x	—	—	—	—	—	x	Served in 4th M.I.
2397	Sergeant A. Couldrey ...	x	x	x	x	x	x	—	—	—	—	—	x	Served with 4th M.I. Mentioned in Despatches. Awarded the Distinguished Conduct Medal.
5237	Corporal F. Caulfield ...	x	x	x	—	—	—	—	—	—	—	—	—	
4016	Sergeant T. Chester ...	x	x	x	x	x	x	—	—	—	—	—	x	
3516	Col.-Sergeant J. Clifford	x	x	—	—	—	—	—	—	x	—	—	x	
7370	Col.-Sergeant W. Coates	—	—	—	—	—	—	x	x	x	—	—	—	Volunteer Service Company.
2898	Corporal G. Collings ...	x	x	x	—	—	—	—	—	—	—	—	—	Mentioned in Despatches. Awarded the Distinguished Conduct Medal. Died at Deelfontein.
3188	Corporal H. J. Collings	x	x	x	x	x	x	—	—	—	—	—	x	

No.	Name	1	2	3	4	5	6	7	8	9	10	11	12	Remarks
			Served with 4th M.I.	Volunteer Service Company.			Served with 2nd M.I. Mentioned in Despatches. Clasp for Wittebergen.				Wounded at Kitchener's Kop.	Died at Bloemfontein.	Promoted Sergeant-Major in 3rd Battalion.	
3152	Corporal T. Conroy	X				X		X			X	X		X
1868	Sergeant T. Cordell						X			X				
7310	Sergeant A. E. Crosier		X		X	X								
3222	Corporal T. Crouch	X					X			X		X		
4159	Col.-Sergt. W. Cushen		X	X										
5073	Sergeant L. Davies		X	X							X			
4688	Sergeant J. Davis				X			X	X	X				X
3911	Sergeant M. Delaney		X	X	X	X		X	X	X				X
4313	Sergeant W. J. Dimond		X					X	X	X				X
1668	Sergeant J. Dixon	X			X	X	X	X		X		X	X	
4524	Sergeant S. Driscoll	X			X	X		X	X		X	X		
4038	Sergeant A. Dutfield	X			X	X	X	X	X		X	X		X
3657	Corporal W. G. Dunn													
1303	Corporal T. Duffy													
213	Qr.-Mstr. Sergeant S. C. Eastwood													

158

APPENDIX H.—ROLL OF WARRANT AND NON-COMMISSIONED OFFICERS, SHEWING RANK HELD AT END OF WAR.

Regimental Number.	Rank and Name.	Queen's Medal and Clasps.											King's Medal.	Remarks.
		Relief of Kimberley.	Paardeberg.	Driefontein.	Johannesburg.	Diamond Hill.	Belfast.	Cape Colony.	Orange Free State.	Transvaal.	South Africa, 1901.	South Africa, 1902.		
3548	Sergeant R. Edwards...	—	—	—	—	—	—	—	—	x	—	x	—	
4802	Sergt. G. Fairweather...	x	—	—	—	x	x	x	x	—	—	—	x	
5757	Corporal H. Fane ...	x	x	x	—	x	x	—	—	—	—	—	x	
5410	Lce.-Sergt. J. Fannon...	x	x	—	—	x	x	—	—	—	—	—	x	
5329	Lce.-Sergt. D. Featonby	x	x	x	x	x	x	x	x	—	—	—	—	
7267	Sergt. J. J. Fishbourne	—	—	x	—	x	x	—	x	—	—	—	—	
1162	Lc.-Sergt. P. Fitzgerald	x	x	—	x	—	—	x	—	x	—	—	x	
5829	Corporal G. H. Fleming	x	x	x	x	x	x	x	x	—	—	—	x	
3930	Corporal J. Foster ...	—	—	x	x	x	x	—	—	—	—	—	—	
1233	Corporal F. Frankland	x	x	—	—	—	x	—	—	—	—	—	—	
2820	Sergt.-Dr. T. Fraser ...	x	x	x	x	x	x	—	—	—	—	—	x	Killed at Paardeberg.
3902	Corporal H. Gibson ...	—	—	—	—	—	—	—	—	x	—	x	—	

												Died at Deelfontein.			Officers' Mess Sergeant.
2793	Sergeant T. Gill …		x				x	x				x					x
5564	Corporal T. C. Goode			x	x	x					x					x	
4773	Sergeant F. Goozee …				x	x			x	x	x				x	x	
4113	Sergeant R. Gordon …			x	x	x	x				x	x				x	
4354	Sergeant C. S. Graham										x					x	
4685	Sergeant-Master-Tailor W. H. Gregg										x		x			x	
4693	Sergeant G. Green …		x					x	x	x					x		
5199	Sergt. R. Greenhough…		x					x	x	x					x		
2580	Corporal F. Grey …	x	x					x	x	x					x		x
4035	Corporal A. Gundry …	x	x				x	x	x			x		x	x		x
3090	Corporal W. F. Hall …	x	x				x	x	x	x		x		x	x		x
2697	Band-Sergt. W. F. Hall	x	x				x	x	x	x		x		x	x		x

160

APPENDIX H.—ROLL OF WARRANT AND NON-COMMISSIONED OFFICERS, SHEWING RANK HELD AT END OF WAR.

Regimental Number	Rank and Name	Queen's Medal and Clasps.											King's Medal.	Remarks.
		Relief of Kimberley	Paardeberg	Driefontein	Johannesburg	Diamond Hill	Belfast	Cape Colony	Orange Free State	Transvaal	South Africa 1901	South Africa 1902		
3677	Corporal E. Hasker ...	×	×	×	×	×	×						×	Wounded at Driefontein.
3620	Sergeant F. C. Hatton	×	×	×										
5684	Sergeant A. P. Hatton	×	×							×			×	Wounded at Paardeberg. Twice mentioned in Despatches. Promoted Corporal for Distinguished Conduct.
5910	Corporal H. Harrison...	×	×	×	×	×	×						×	Served with 4th M.I.
3792	Sergeant W. Heald ...	×	×							×			×	
4608	Corporal S. Hawkins ...				×	×	×	×	×				×	Served with 4th M.I.
1319	Corporal E. Henderson	×	×											Wounded at Paardeberg.
3187	Corporal J. Henderson	×	×	×	×	×	×				×		×	Served with 21st M.I. and 4th M.I.
5104	Corporal J. R. Hey ...							×		×				
3153	Corporal H. T. Hinde...							×	×	×	×	×		

161

No.	Name	Notes
3370	Sergeant J. W. Higham	Acting Sergeant-Major 3rd Railway Pioneer Regiment. Served with 4th M.I.
5401	Lce.-Sergt. A. E. Hope	
4170	Sergt. N. W. Hopkins	
3373	Sergeant R. Hopkins ...	
5537	Corpl. L. Hollingshead	
3315	Pr.-Sergt. W. P. Hough	
3267	Sergeant T. Houghton	
4039	Col.-Sergt. H. Howe ...	
3920	Col.-Sergt. P. Hughes	Killed at Paardeberg.
5102	Sergeant E. Humphries	Served with 4th M.I. Specially mentioned in Battalion Orders for good work.
5837	Corpl. A. E. Hutchins	
3098	Sergeant J. P. Hyland	Served with 4th M.I. Mentioned in Despatches. Awarded the Distinguished Conduct Medal.
2682	Corporal J. Jackson ...	
5156	Lce.-Sergt. D. Jamieson	Killed at Slingersfontein.
4756	Sergeant W. Jessop ...	
5184	Sergeant D. Johnson ...	

162

APPENDIX H.—ROLL OF WARRANT AND NON-COMMISSIONED OFFICERS, SHEWING RANK HELD AT END OF WAR.

Regimental Number.	Rank and Name.	Queen's Medal and Clasps.											King's Medal.	Remarks.
		Relief of Kimberley.	Paardeberg.	Driefontein.	Johannesburg.	Diamond Hill.	Belfast.	Cape Colony.	Orange Free State.	Transvaal.	South Africa, 1901.	South Africa, 1902.		
2370	Sergeant J. Johnson …	×	×	×	—	—	—	—	—	—	—	—	—	
5615	Corpl. W. W. Jones …	×	×	×	×	×	×	—	—	—	—	—	×	
5997	Corporal W. Kaye …	×	×	×	×	×	×	—	—	—	—	—	×	
5430	Corporal H. Kaye …	×	×	×	×	—	—	—	—	—	—	—	—	
2409	Sergeant T. D. Kear …	×	×	×	×	×	—	—	—	—	—	—	—	
3231	Corporal J. H. Kearns	×	×	—	—	—	—	—	—	—	—	—	—	Killed at Paardeberg.
4633	Corporal G. H. King …	×	—	—	—	—	—	—	—	×	—	—	×	Wounded at Paardeberg.
4785	Corporal E. T. Lack …	—	—	—	—	—	—	—	—	×	—	×	—	
7244	Sergeant R. Lambert …	—	—	—	—	—	—	—	—	—	—	—	—	
3940	Sergeant W. Larmer …	×	×	×	×	×	×	×	×	—	×	—	—	Served with 4th M.I.
7270	Corporal G. J. Lawn …	—	—	—	×	×	×	×	×	—	—	—	—	
6222	Corporal W. Leonard…	—	—	—	—	—	—	×	×	×	—	—	×	Volunteer Service Company.

No.	Name							Served with 4th and 21st M.I.	Served with 4th M.I.			Wounded at Driefontein.	Mentioned in Despatches.	Volunteer Service Company.
4930	Corporal W. Lennan	—	×	×	×	×	×	×	—	×	×	×	×	—	—
5386	Corporal S. Leith	×	—	—	—	—	—	—	—	—	—	—	—	—	×
5055	Corporal F. J. Lilley	×	—	—	—	—	—	—	—	—	—	—	—	×	—
5340	Corporal H. Lindley	×	×	×	—	—	—	×	×	—	—	—	—	—	×
821	Corporal T. Little	×	—	—	—	—	—	×	—	×	—	—	—	—	—
3386	Sergeant J. P. Long	×	—	—	—	—	—	×	—	×	—	—	—	—	—
4867	Corporal R. Lovatt	—	—	—	×	×	×	—	—	×	×	×	×	—	×
5283	Sergeant J. Lowther	—	—	—	×	×	×	—	—	×	×	×	×	—	×
3407	Col.-Sgt. H. S. Mackay	—	×	—	×	×	×	—	—	×	—	—	×	×	—
7372	Sergeant C. McKenzie	—	×	×	×	×	×	—	—	×	×	×	×	×	—
4392	Corpl. W. G. McFadyen	—	×	×	×	×	×	—	—	×	×	×	×	×	—
4211	Corporal A. McHugh														
3392	Corporal W. McFarlane														
5522	Corporal R. G. Manlove														
4735	Lnce.-Sergt. W. Mann														
3914	Sergeant J. Mathers														

APPENDIX H.—ROLL OF WARRANT AND NON-COMMISSIONED OFFICERS, SHEWING RANK HELD AT END OF WAR.

Regimental Number.	Rank and Name.	Queen's Medal and Clasps.											King's Medal.	Remarks.
		Relief of Kimberley	Paardeberg	Driefontein	Johannesburg	Diamond Hill	Belfast	Cape Colony	Orange Free State	Transvaal	South Africa, 1901.	South Africa, 1902.		
2856	Corporal G. H. Mee ...	x	x	x	x	x	x	—	—	—	—	—	x	
874	Sergt. W. Middlewood	x	x	x	x	x	x	—	—	—	x	—	—	
2772	Lnce.-Sergeant Milburn	x	x	x	x	x	x	—	—	—	x	—	—	Served with 4th M.I. Promoted Lance-Sergeant for good work at Joubert's Houghte, April 14th, 1901.
3429	Sergeant W. Miller ...	—	—	—	x	x	—	x	x	x	x	x	—	
4652	Corporal L. Moorhouse	—	—	—	x	x	—	x	x	x	x	x	—	
4162	Sergeant G. Morley ...	x	x	x	x	x	x	—	—	—	—	—	x	
3347	Corporal J. Nagginton	x	x	x	x	x	x	—	—	—	x	—	—	
3780	Lce.-Sergt. J. Nicholson	x	x	x	x	x	x	—	—	—	—	—	x	Served with 4th M.I. Died at Middleburg, Transvaal.
5082	Sergeant J. O'Brien ...	x	x	x	x	x	x	—	—	—	x	—	—	
1521	Corporal G. Parker ...	x	x	x	x	x	x	—	—	—	x	x	—	
6136	Corporal W. Parkin ...	—	—	—	—	—	—	—	—	x	x	x	—	Served with 4th M.I.

No.	Name												Remarks
4548	Sergeant H. Parkinson	x	—	—	—	—	—	x	x	x	x	x	Served with 4th M.I. Mentioned in Despatches. Awarded the Distinguished Conduct Medal.
5117	Corporal J. M. Paton	x	—	—	—	—	—	x	x	x	x	x	Served with 2nd M.I.
3472	Col.-Sergt. E. Pickard	x	—	—	—	—	—	x	x	x	x	x	Mentioned in Despatches. Awarded the Distinguished Conduct Medal.
3221	Corporal J. Pearson	x	—	—	—	x	x	x	x	—	—	—	
3237	Corporal T. Pennington	—	—	—	—	—	—	—	—	x	x	x	
2675	Corporal W. Philpott	—	—	—	—	—	—	x	x	x	x	x	Mentioned in Despatches. Awarded the Distinguished Conduct Medal.
5878	Corporal A. Pollard	x	—	—	x	—	—	x	x	x	x	—	
5530	Corporal F. Rabey	x	—	—	—	—	—	x	x	—	—	x	
4483	Corporal C. Rayner	—	—	—	—	—	—	—	—	—	—	—	
3549	Sergeant B. Richardson	x	—	—	—	—	—	x	x	x	x	x	Twice mentioned in Despatches. Killed at Kitchener's Kop.
3537	Corpl. J. W. Richardson	—	—	—	—	—	—	—	—	—	—	—	
4960	Sergt. W. T. Richardson	x	—	—	x	—	—	x	x	x	x	x	
1812	Sergeant C. Richens	—	—	—	—	—	—	—	—	—	x	—	
3416	Col.-Sergt. F. Roberts	x	—	—	—	—	—	—	—	—	—	—	Killed at Slingersfontein.
3433	Corporal W. Roberts	x	—	—	—	—	—	x	x	x	x	x	

APPENDIX H.—ROLL OF WARRANT AND NON-COMMISSIONED OFFICERS, SHEWING RANK HELD AT END OF WAR.

Regimental Number	Rank and Name	Queen's Medal and Clasps.											King's Medal.	Remarks.
		Relief of Kimberley.	Paardeberg.	Driefontein.	Johannesburg.	Diamond Hill.	Belfast.	Cape Colony.	Orange Free State.	Transvaal.	South Africa, 1901.	South Africa, 1902.		
3055	Col.-Sergt. J. Robinson	x	x	x	—	—	x	—	—	—	—	—	x	
3533	Corporal W. Robinson	x	x	—	—	—	—	—	—	—	—	—	—	
5729	Corporal H. Rounce ...	x	x	x	—	x	x	—	—	—	—	—	x	
5171	Corporal H. Rowe ...	x	x	x	—	—	x	—	—	—	—	—	x	
2576	Sergeant W. Sandford	x	x	x	—	—	—	—	—	x	—	—	—	
1207	Sergeant E. H. Scarborough	—	—	—	—	—	—	x	x	x	—	—	—	
604	Sergeant-Instructor J. W. Scarborough	—	—	—	x	x	x	x	x	—	—	—	—	Served with 4th M.I. Mentioned in despatches.
4710	Corpl. T. W. Schofield	x	x	—	x	x	x	x	x	—	—	—	x	
4302	Corporal F. Scholes ...	—	—	—	—	—	—	—	—	x	x	x	—	
2780	Corporal W. Schollhamer	—	—	—	—	—	—	x	x	x	—	—	x	

5920	Corporal F. Slack	...	I	I	—	—	I	I	I	I	I	I	I	I
4026	Corporal J. Slinn	...	I	I	—	I	I	I	—	I	I	I	—	I
2913	Sergeant R. Southern	... Volunteer Service Company.	I	I	—	I	I	I	I	—	—	I	I	I
7285	Corporal H. Smith	...	I	I	I	I	I	—	—	I	I	I	—	I
5835	Corporal Simpson	...	—	I	I	—	—	I	I	—	I	—	I	I
5929	Corporal J. Stalker	...	—	I	I	—	—	I	I	—	—	I	I	I
5267	Sergeant W. Stalker	... Wounded at Paardeberg.	I	I	I	I	—	—	I	—	—	I	—	I
2584	Sergeant H. Stanley	...	I	—	I	—	—	—	I	I	—	—	—	—	I
1275	Corporal F. E. Stevens	...	I	—	I	—	—	—	I	—	—	—	—	I	I
2557	Corporal G. Stevens	... Volunteer Service Company.	I	I	—	I	I	I	—	I	—	—	I	I
7324	Corporal A. Stephenson	...	I	—	—	I	I	—	I	—	—	—	I	—	—
3630	Corporal H. Stocker	...	I	—	—	I	I	I	I	—	I	—	I	—	—
2964	Corporal C. Summers	...	I	—	I	—	I	I	—	—	—	—	—	—	—

APPENDIX H.—ROLL OF WARRANT AND NON-COMMISSIONED OFFICERS, SHEWING RANK HELD AT END OF WAR.

Regimental Number	Rank and Name	Queen's Medal and Clasps.											King's Medal.	Remarks.
		Relief of Kimberley	Paardeberg	Driefontein	Johannesburg	Diamond Hill	Belfast	Cape Colony	Orange Free State	Transvaal	South Africa, 1901	South Africa, 1902		
6116	Corporal L. Sykes	–	–	–	–	–	–	1	1	–	–	–	1	Served with 4th M.I.
3285	Sergeant E. Talling	1	1	1	1	1	1	–	–	–	–	–	1	
3160	Sergeant R. Tate	1	1	1	–	–	–	–	–	–	1	–	–	Killed at Paardeberg.
3254	Sergeant F. Taylor	1	–	1	1	1	–	–	–	–	–	–	–	
4215	Sergeant T. Taylor	1	1	–	–	–	1	–	–	–	–	–	1	
5365	Corporal W. Taylor	1	1	1	1	–	–	–	–	–	–	–	–	Wounded at Kitchener's Kop.
5654	Corporal T. Taylor	1	1	1	1	1	1	–	–	–	–	–	1	
4639	Corporal G. Taylor	–	1	1	1	1	1	–	–	1	1	–	–	
5577	Corporal G. Temple	1	1	1	–	1	1	–	–	–	–	–	1	
3424	Q.-Mstr. Sergeant W. Thirkell	1	1	–	–	–	1	–	–	–	–	–	1	
3475	Sergt. A. E. Thompson	1	1	1	1	1	1	–	–	–	–	–	1	

No.	Name	1	2	3	4	5	6	7	8	9	10	11	12	13	Remarks
3973	Sergeant M. A. Thomson						x	x	x	x		x			x	
1287	Sergeant J. Thompson	x			x	x										x
1660	Sergeant R. Thompson				x	x					x					
6366	Corporal G. Thornton	x			x	x		x		x						x
4966	Corporal M. Thwaites				x					x			x			x
4329	Sergeant A. Tomkins			x	x								x	x	x	x
3626	Corporal A. Tribe						x		x		x	x		x			Served with 4th M.I. Died on passage home.
4263	Sergeant J. Tripp		x				x		x		x	x		x			Transport Sergeant.
5734	Corporal H. Vennison		x			x		x		x	x		x				Wounded at Paardeberg.
3313	Col.-Sergeant E. Wall		x			x	x	x		x	x	x				
2367	Sergt.-Major J. Walker		x			x	x	x	x	x	x						Signalling Sergeant.
3033	Sergeant J. Walsh															
7327	Corporal J. C. Ward															
3689	Q.-Mstr.-Sergeant C. Watmuff															
3017	Col.-Sergeant W. Weare															
5180	Corporal H. E. Webb															

170

APPENDIX H.—ROLL OF WARRANT AND NON-COMMISSIONED OFFICERS, SHEWING RANK HELD AT END OF WAR.

Regimental Number	Rank and Name	Relief of Kimberley	Paardeberg	Driefontein	Johannesburg	Diamond Hill	Belfast	Cape Colony	Orange Free State	Transvaal	South Africa, 1901.	South Africa, 1902.	King's Medal	Remarks
3702	Sergeant G. Webster	—	—	—	—	—	—	1	1	1	—	1	—	
3325	Corporal M. Welford	1	1	1	1	1	—	—	—	—	—	—	1	
4596	Sergeant G. Welch	—	—	—	—	—	1	1	1	1	—	—	1	
4747	Corporal G. Wedge	—	—	—	—	—	—	1	1	1	—	—	1	
3283	Sergt. T. H. Wheatley	1	1	—	1	1	1	—	—	—	1	—	—	
4156	Sergeant B. Whelan	1	1	1	1	1	1	—	—	—	1	—	—	
4916	Corporal W. Wiles	1	1	—	—	—	—	—	—	—	—	—	—	Wounded at Paardeberg. Died at Netley.
3961	Col.-Sergt. B. Williams	1	—	1	1	1	1	—	—	—	—	—	1	Mentioned in Despatches. Awarded the Distinguished Conduct Medal.
3493	Sergeant H. F. Wilson	1	1	1	1	1	1	—	—	—	—	—	1	
4157	Sergeant H. W. Wilson	1	1	1	1	1	—	—	—	—	—	—	1	Served with 2nd M.I. Mentioned in Despatches. Awarded the Distinguished Conduct Medal. Clasp for Wittebergen.

No.	Name										Remarks
3056	Sergeant J. Windham...	x	x	x	x	x	—	—	—	—	x
4323	Sergeant W. J. Wise ...	x	x	—	—	—	x	—	—	—	x
3937	Sergeant G. H. Wolpert	x	x	x	—	—	—	—	—	—	—
5376	Sergeant W. Wood ...	x	—	—	x	x	—	—	—	—	x
5392	Corporal G. Woodhead	x	x	—	—	—	—	—	—	—	x	Served with 4th M.I. Wounded at Driefontein.
4646	Sergeant J. H. Wright	x	x	—	—	—	—	—	—	—	—	Served with 21st M.I.
892	Sergeant E. Yates ...	x	x	—	x	x	—	—	x	—	—

ALSO FROM LEONAUR
AVAILABLE IN SOFTCOVER OR HARDCOVER WITH DUST JACKET

AFGHANISTAN: THE BELEAGUERED BRIGADE *by G. R. Gleig*—An Account of Sale's Brigade During the First Afghan War.

IN THE RANKS OF THE C. I. V *by Erskine Childers*—With the City Imperial Volunteer Battery (Honourable Artillery Company) in the Second Boer War.

THE BENGAL NATIVE ARMY *by F. G. Cardew*—An Invaluable Reference Resource.

THE 7TH (QUEEN'S OWN) HUSSARS: Volume 4—1688-1914 *by C. R. B. Barrett*—Uniforms, Equipment, Weapons, Traditions, the Services of Notable Officers and Men & the Appendices to All Volumes—Volume 4: 1688-1914.

THE SWORD OF THE CROWN *by Eric W. Sheppard*—A History of the British Army to 1914.

THE 7TH (QUEEN'S OWN) HUSSARS: Volume 3—**1818-1914** *by C. R. B. Barrett*—On Campaign During the Canadian Rebellion, the Indian Mutiny, the Sudan, Matabeleland, Mashonaland and the Boer War Volume 3: 1818-1914.

THE KHARTOUM CAMPAIGN *by Bennet Burleigh*—A Special Correspondent's View of the Reconquest of the Sudan by British and Egyptian Forces under Kitchener—1898.

EL PUCHERO *by Richard McSherry*—The Letters of a Surgeon of Volunteers During Scott's Campaign of the American-Mexican War 1847-1848.

RIFLEMAN SAHIB *by E. Maude*—The Recollections of an Officer of the Bombay Rifles During the Southern Mahratta Campaign, Second Sikh War, Persian Campaign and Indian Mutiny.

THE KING'S HUSSAR *by Edwin Mole*—The Recollections of a 14th (King's) Hussar During the Victorian Era.

JOHN COMPANY'S CAVALRYMAN *by William Johnson*—The Experiences of a British Soldier in the Crimea, the Persian Campaign and the Indian Mutiny.

COLENSO & DURNFORD'S ZULU WAR *by Frances E. Colenso & Edward Durnford*—The first and possibly the most important history of the Zulu War.

U. S. DRAGOON *by Samuel E. Chamberlain*—Experiences in the Mexican War 1846-48 and on the South Western Frontier.

AVAILABLE ONLINE AT www.leonaur.com
AND FROM ALL GOOD BOOK STORES

ALSO FROM LEONAUR
AVAILABLE IN SOFTCOVER OR HARDCOVER WITH DUST JACKET

THE 2ND MAORI WAR: 1860-1861 *by Robert Carey*—The Second Maori War, or First Taranaki War, one more bloody instalment of the conflicts between European settlers and the indigenous Maori people.

A JOURNAL OF THE SECOND SIKH WAR *by Daniel A. Sandford*—The Experiences of an Ensign of the 2nd Bengal European Regiment During the Campaign in the Punjab, India, 1848-49.

THE LIGHT INFANTRY OFFICER *by John H. Cooke*—The Experiences of an Officer of the 43rd Light Infantry in America During the War of 1812.

BUSHVELDT CARBINEERS *by George Witton*—The War Against the Boers in South Africa and the 'Breaker' Morant Incident.

LAKE'S CAMPAIGNS IN INDIA *by Hugh Pearse*—The Second Anglo Maratha War, 1803-1807.

BRITAIN IN AFGHANISTAN 1: THE FIRST AFGHAN WAR 1839-42 *by Archibald Forbes*—From invasion to destruction-a British military disaster.

BRITAIN IN AFGHANISTAN 2: THE SECOND AFGHAN WAR 1878-80 *by Archibald Forbes*—This is the history of the Second Afghan War-another episode of British military history typified by savagery, massacre, siege and battles.

UP AMONG THE PANDIES *by Vivian Dering Majendie*—Experiences of a British Officer on Campaign During the Indian Mutiny, 1857-1858.

MUTINY: 1857 *by James Humphries*—Authentic Voices from the Indian Mutiny-First Hand Accounts of Battles, Sieges and Personal Hardships.

BLOW THE BUGLE, DRAW THE SWORD *by W. H. G. Kingston*—The Wars, Campaigns, Regiments and Soldiers of the British & Indian Armies During the Victorian Era, 1839-1898.

WAR BEYOND THE DRAGON PAGODA *by Major J. J. Snodgrass*—A Personal Narrative of the First Anglo-Burmese War 1824 - 1826.

THE HERO OF ALIWAL *by James Humphries*—The Campaigns of Sir Harry Smith in India, 1843-1846, During the Gwalior War & the First Sikh War.

ALL FOR A SHILLING A DAY *by Donald F. Featherstone*—The story of H.M. 16th, the Queen's Lancers During the first Sikh War 1845-1846.

AVAILABLE ONLINE AT www.leonaur.com
AND FROM ALL GOOD BOOK STORES

ALSO FROM LEONAUR
AVAILABLE IN SOFTCOVER OR HARDCOVER WITH DUST JACKET

THE FALL OF THE MOGHUL EMPIRE OF HINDUSTAN by *H. G. Keene*—By the beginning of the nineteenth century, as British and Indian armies under Lake and Wellesley dominated the scene, a little over half a century of conflict brought the Moghul Empire to its knees.

LADY SALE'S AFGHANISTAN by *Florentia Sale*—An Indomitable Victorian Lady's Account of the Retreat from Kabul During the First Afghan War.

THE CAMPAIGN OF MAGENTA AND SOLFERINO 1859 by *Harold Carmichael Wylly*—The Decisive Conflict for the Unification of Italy.

FRENCH'S CAVALRY CAMPAIGN by *J. G. Maydon*—A Special Correspondent's View of British Army Mounted Troops During the Boer War.

CAVALRY AT WATERLOO by *Sir Evelyn Wood*—British Mounted Troops During the Campaign of 1815.

THE SUBALTERN by *George Robert Gleig*—The Experiences of an Officer of the 85th Light Infantry During the Peninsular War.

NAPOLEON AT BAY, 1814 by *F. Loraine Petre*—The Campaigns to the Fall of the First Empire.

NAPOLEON AND THE CAMPAIGN OF 1806 by *Colonel Vachée*—The Napoleonic Method of Organisation and Command to the Battles of Jena & Auerstädt.

THE COMPLETE ADVENTURES IN THE CONNAUGHT RANGERS by *William Grattan*—The 88th Regiment during the Napoleonic Wars by a Serving Officer.

BUGLER AND OFFICER OF THE RIFLES by *William Green & Harry Smith*—With the 95th (Rifles) during the Peninsular & Waterloo Campaigns of the Napoleonic Wars.

NAPOLEONIC WAR STORIES by *Sir Arthur Quiller-Couch*—Tales of soldiers, spies, battles & sieges from the Peninsular & Waterloo campaigns.

CAPTAIN OF THE 95TH (RIFLES) by *Jonathan Leach*—An officer of Wellington's sharpshooters during the Peninsular, South of France and Waterloo campaigns of the Napoleonic wars.

RIFLEMAN COSTELLO by *Edward Costello*—The adventures of a soldier of the 95th (Rifles) in the Peninsular & Waterloo Campaigns of the Napoleonic wars.

AVAILABLE ONLINE AT **www.leonaur.com**
AND FROM ALL GOOD BOOK STORES

ALSO FROM LEONAUR
AVAILABLE IN SOFTCOVER OR HARDCOVER WITH DUST JACKET

AT THEM WITH THE BAYONET *by Donald F. Featherstone*—The first Anglo-Sikh War 1845-1846.

STEPHEN CRANE'S BATTLES *by Stephen Crane*—Nine Decisive Battles Recounted by the Author of 'The Red Badge of Courage'.

THE GURKHA WAR *by H. T. Prinsep*—The Anglo-Nepalese Conflict in North East India 1814-1816.

FIRE & BLOOD *by G. R. Gleig*—The burning of Washington & the battle of New Orleans, 1814, through the eyes of a young British soldier.

SOUND ADVANCE! *by Joseph Anderson*—Experiences of an officer of HM 50th regiment in Australia, Burma & the Gwalior war.

THE CAMPAIGN OF THE INDUS *by Thomas Holdsworth*—Experiences of a British Officer of the 2nd (Queen's Royal) Regiment in the Campaign to Place Shah Shuja on the Throne of Afghanistan 1838 - 1840.

WITH THE MADRAS EUROPEAN REGIMENT IN BURMA *by John Butler*—The Experiences of an Officer of the Honourable East India Company's Army During the First Anglo-Burmese War 1824 - 1826.

IN ZULULAND WITH THE BRITISH ARMY *by Charles L. Norris-Newman*—The Anglo-Zulu war of 1879 through the first-hand experiences of a special correspondent.

BESIEGED IN LUCKNOW *by Martin Richard Gubbins*—The first Anglo-Sikh War 1845-1846.

A TIGER ON HORSEBACK *by L. March Phillips*—The Experiences of a Trooper & Officer of Rimington's Guides - The Tigers - during the Anglo-Boer war 1899 - 1902.

SEPOYS, SIEGE & STORM *by Charles John Griffiths*—The Experiences of a young officer of H.M.'s 61st Regiment at Ferozepore, Delhi ridge and at the fall of Delhi during the Indian mutiny 1857.

CAMPAIGNING IN ZULULAND *by W. E. Montague*—Experiences on campaign during the Zulu war of 1879 with the 94th Regiment.

THE STORY OF THE GUIDES *by G.J. Younghusband*—The Exploits of the Soldiers of the famous Indian Army Regiment from the northwest frontier 1847 - 1900.

AVAILABLE ONLINE AT **www.leonaur.com**
AND FROM ALL GOOD BOOK STORES

ALSO FROM LEONAUR
AVAILABLE IN SOFTCOVER OR HARDCOVER WITH DUST JACKET

ZULU:1879 by *D.C.F. Moodie & the Leonaur Editors*—The Anglo-Zulu War of 1879 from contemporary sources: First Hand Accounts, Interviews, Dispatches, Official Documents & Newspaper Reports.

THE RED DRAGOON by *W.J. Adams*—With the 7th Dragoon Guards in the Cape of Good Hope against the Boers & the Kaffir tribes during the 'war of the axe' 1843-48'.

THE RECOLLECTIONS OF SKINNER OF SKINNER'S HORSE by *James Skinner*—James Skinner and his 'Yellow Boys' Irregular cavalry in the wars of India between the British, Mahratta, Rajput, Mogul, Sikh & Pindarree Forces.

A CAVALRY OFFICER DURING THE SEPOY REVOLT by *A. R. D. Mackenzie*—Experiences with the 3rd Bengal Light Cavalry, the Guides and Sikh Irregular Cavalry from the outbreak to Delhi and Lucknow.

A NORFOLK SOLDIER IN THE FIRST SIKH WAR by *J W Baldwin*—Experiences of a private of H.M. 9th Regiment of Foot in the battles for the Punjab, India 1845-6.

TOMMY ATKINS' WAR STORIES: 14 FIRST HAND ACCOUNTS—Fourteen first hand accounts from the ranks of the British Army during Queen Victoria's Empire.

THE WATERLOO LETTERS by *H. T. Siborne*—Accounts of the Battle by British Officers for its Foremost Historian.

NEY: GENERAL OF CAVALRY VOLUME 1—1769-1799 by *Antoine Bulos*—The Early Career of a Marshal of the First Empire.

NEY: MARSHAL OF FRANCE VOLUME 2—1799-1805 by *Antoine Bulos*—The Early Career of a Marshal of the First Empire.

AIDE-DE-CAMP TO NAPOLEON by *Philippe-Paul de Ségur*—For anyone interested in the Napoleonic Wars this book, written by one who was intimate with the strategies and machinations of the Emperor, will be essential reading.

TWILIGHT OF EMPIRE by *Sir Thomas Ussher & Sir George Cockburn*—Two accounts of Napoleon's Journeys in Exile to Elba and St. Helena: Narrative of Events by Sir Thomas Ussher & Napoleon's Last Voyage: Extract of a diary by Sir George Cockburn.

PRIVATE WHEELER by *William Wheeler*—The letters of a soldier of the 51st Light Infantry during the Peninsular War & at Waterloo.

AVAILABLE ONLINE AT www.leonaur.com
AND FROM ALL GOOD BOOK STORES

ALSO FROM LEONAUR
AVAILABLE IN SOFTCOVER OR HARDCOVER WITH DUST JACKET

OFFICERS & GENTLEMEN *by Peter Hawker & William Graham*—Two Accounts of British Officers During the Peninsula War: Officer of Light Dragoons by Peter Hawker & Campaign in Portugal and Spain by William Graham.

THE WALCHEREN EXPEDITION *by Anonymous*—The Experiences of a British Officer of the 81st Regt. During the Campaign in the Low Countries of 1809.

LADIES OF WATERLOO *by Charlotte A. Eaton, Magdalene de Lancey & Juana Smith*—The Experiences of Three Women During the Campaign of 1815: Waterloo Days by Charlotte A. Eaton, A Week at Waterloo by Magdalene de Lancey & Juana's Story by Juana Smith.

JOURNAL OF AN OFFICER IN THE KING'S GERMAN LEGION *by John Frederick Hering*—Recollections of Campaigning During the Napoleonic Wars.

JOURNAL OF AN ARMY SURGEON IN THE PENINSULAR WAR *by Charles Boutflower*—The Recollections of a British Army Medical Man on Campaign During the Napoleonic Wars.

ON CAMPAIGN WITH MOORE AND WELLINGTON *by Anthony Hamilton*—The Experiences of a Soldier of the 43rd Regiment During the Peninsular War.

THE ROAD TO AUSTERLITZ *by R. G. Burton*—Napoleon's Campaign of 1805.

SOLDIERS OF NAPOLEON *by A. J. Doisy De Villargennes & Arthur Chuquet*—The Experiences of the Men of the French First Empire: Under the Eagles by A. J. Doisy De Villargennes & Voices of 1812 by Arthur Chuquet.

INVASION OF FRANCE, 1814 *by F. W. O. Maycock*—The Final Battles of the Napoleonic First Empire.

LEIPZIG—A CONFLICT OF TITANS *by Frederic Shoberl*—A Personal Experience of the 'Battle of the Nations' During the Napoleonic Wars, October 14th-19th, 1813.

SLASHERS *by Charles Cadell*—The Campaigns of the 28th Regiment of Foot During the Napoleonic Wars by a Serving Officer.

BATTLE IMPERIAL *by Charles William Vane*—The Campaigns in Germany & France for the Defeat of Napoleon 1813-1814.

SWIFT & BOLD *by Gibbes Rigaud*—The 60th Rifles During the Peninsula War.

ALSO FROM LEONAUR
AVAILABLE IN SOFTCOVER OR HARDCOVER WITH DUST JACKET

ADVENTURES OF A YOUNG RIFLEMAN *by Johann Christian Maempel*—The Experiences of a Saxon in the French & British Armies During the Napoleonic Wars.

THE HUSSAR *by Norbert Landsheit & G. R. Gleig*—A German Cavalryman in British Service Throughout the Napoleonic Wars.

RECOLLECTIONS OF THE PENINSULA *by Moyle Sherer*—An Officer of the 34th Regiment of Foot—'The Cumberland Gentlemen'—on Campaign Against Napoleon's French Army in Spain.

MARINE OF REVOLUTION & CONSULATE *by Moreau de Jonnès*—The Recollections of a French Soldier of the Revolutionary Wars 1791-1804.

GENTLEMEN IN RED *by John Dobbs & Robert Knowles*—Two Accounts of British Infantry Officers During the Peninsular War Recollections of an Old 52nd Man by John Dobbs An Officer of Fusiliers by Robert Knowles.

CORPORAL BROWN'S CAMPAIGNS IN THE LOW COUNTRIES *by Robert Brown*—Recollections of a Coldstream Guard in the Early Campaigns Against Revolutionary France 1793-1795.

THE 7TH (QUEENS OWN) HUSSARS: Volume 2—1793-1815 *by C. R. B. Barrett*—During the Campaigns in the Low Countries & the Peninsula and Waterloo Campaigns of the Napoleonic Wars. Volume 2: 1793-1815.

THE MARENGO CAMPAIGN 1800 *by Herbert H. Sargent*—The Victory that Completed the Austrian Defeat in Italy.

DONALDSON OF THE 94TH—SCOTS BRIGADE *by Joseph Donaldson*—The Recollections of a Soldier During the Peninsula & South of France Campaigns of the Napoleonic Wars.

A CONSCRIPT FOR EMPIRE *by Philippe as told to Johann Christian Maempel*—The Experiences of a Young German Conscript During the Napoleonic Wars.

JOURNAL OF THE CAMPAIGN OF 1815 *by Alexander Cavalié Mercer*—The Experiences of an Officer of the Royal Horse Artillery During the Waterloo Campaign.

NAPOLEON'S CAMPAIGNS IN POLAND 1806-7 *by Robert Wilson*—The campaign in Poland from the Russian side of the conflict.

AVAILABLE ONLINE AT www.leonaur.com
AND FROM ALL GOOD BOOK STORES

ALSO FROM LEONAUR
AVAILABLE IN SOFTCOVER OR HARDCOVER WITH DUST JACKET

OMPTEDA OF THE KING'S GERMAN LEGION *by Christian von Ompteda*—A Hanoverian Officer on Campaign Against Napoleon.

LIEUTENANT SIMMONS OF THE 95TH (RIFLES) *by George Simmons*—Recollections of the Peninsula, South of France & Waterloo Campaigns of the Napoleonic Wars.

A HORSEMAN FOR THE EMPEROR *by Jean Baptiste Gazzola*—A Cavalryman of Napoleon's Army on Campaign Throughout the Napoleonic Wars.

SERGEANT LAWRENCE *by William Lawrence*—With the 40th Regt. of Foot in South America, the Peninsular War & at Waterloo.

CAMPAIGNS WITH THE FIELD TRAIN *by Richard D. Henegan*—Experiences of a British Officer During the Peninsula and Waterloo Campaigns of the Napoleonic Wars.

CAVALRY SURGEON *by S. D. Broughton*—On Campaign Against Napoleon in the Peninsula & South of France During the Napoleonic Wars 1812-1814.

MEN OF THE RIFLES *by Thomas Knight, Henry Curling & Jonathan Leach*—The Reminiscences of Thomas Knight of the 95th (Rifles) by Thomas Knight, Henry Curling's Anecdotes by Henry Curling & The Field Services of the Rifle Brigade from its Formation to Waterloo by Jonathan Leach.

THE ULM CAMPAIGN 1805 *by F. N. Maude*—Napoleon and the Defeat of the Austrian Army During the 'War of the Third Coalition'.

SOLDIERING WITH THE 'DIVISION' *by Thomas Garrety*—The Military Experiences of an Infantryman of the 43rd Regiment During the Napoleonic Wars.

SERGEANT MORRIS OF THE 73RD FOOT *by Thomas Morris*—The Experiences of a British Infantryman During the Napoleonic Wars-Including Campaigns in Germany and at Waterloo.

A VOICE FROM WATERLOO *by Edward Cotton*—The Personal Experiences of a British Cavalryman Who Became a Battlefield Guide and Authority on the Campaign of 1815.

NAPOLEON AND HIS MARSHALS *by J. T. Headley*—The Men of the First Empire.

ALSO FROM LEONAUR
AVAILABLE IN SOFTCOVER OR HARDCOVER WITH DUST JACKET

COLBORNE: A SINGULAR TALENT FOR WAR *by John Colborne*—The Napoleonic Wars Career of One of Wellington's Most Highly Valued Officers in Egypt, Holland, Italy, the Peninsula and at Waterloo.

NAPOLEON'S RUSSIAN CAMPAIGN *by Philippe Henri de Segur*—The Invasion, Battles and Retreat by an Aide-de-Camp on the Emperor's Staff.

WITH THE LIGHT DIVISION *by John H. Cooke*—The Experiences of an Officer of the 43rd Light Infantry in the Peninsula and South of France During the Napoleonic Wars.

WELLINGTON AND THE PYRENEES CAMPAIGN VOLUME I: FROM VITORIA TO THE BIDASSOA *by F. C. Beatson*—The final phase of the campaign in the Iberian Peninsula.

WELLINGTON AND THE INVASION OF FRANCE VOLUME II: THE BIDASSOA TO THE BATTLE OF THE NIVELLE *by F. C. Beatson*—The final phase of the campaign in the Iberian Peninsula.

WELLINGTON AND THE FALL OF FRANCE VOLUME III: THE GAVES AND THE BATTLE OF ORTHEZ *by F. C. Beatson*—The final phase of the campaign in the Iberian Peninsula.

NAPOLEON'S IMPERIAL GUARD: FROM MARENGO TO WATERLOO *by J. T. Headley*—The story of Napoleon's Imperial Guard and the men who commanded them.

BATTLES & SIEGES OF THE PENINSULAR WAR *by W. H. Fitchett*—Corunna, Busaco, Albuera, Ciudad Rodrigo, Badajos, Salamanca, San Sebastian & Others.

SERGEANT GUILLEMARD: THE MAN WHO SHOT NELSON? *by Robert Guillemard*—A Soldier of the Infantry of the French Army of Napoleon on Campaign Throughout Europe.

WITH THE GUARDS ACROSS THE PYRENEES *by Robert Batty*—The Experiences of a British Officer of Wellington's Army During the Battles for the Fall of Napoleonic France, 1813.

A STAFF OFFICER IN THE PENINSULA *by E. W. Buckham*—An Officer of the British Staff Corps Cavalry During the Peninsula Campaign of the Napoleonic Wars.

THE LEIPZIG CAMPAIGN: 1813—NAPOLEON AND THE "BATTLE OF THE NATIONS" *by F. N. Maude*—Colonel Maude's analysis of Napoleon's campaign of 1813 around Leipzig.

ALSO FROM LEONAUR
AVAILABLE IN SOFTCOVER OR HARDCOVER WITH DUST JACKET

BUGEAUD: A PACK WITH A BATON by *Thomas Robert Bugeaud*—The Early Campaigns of a Soldier of Napoleon's Army Who Would Become a Marshal of France.

WATERLOO RECOLLECTIONS by *Frederick Llewellyn*—Rare First Hand Accounts, Letters, Reports and Retellings from the Campaign of 1815.

SERGEANT NICOL by *Daniel Nicol*—The Experiences of a Gordon Highlander During the Napoleonic Wars in Egypt, the Peninsula and France.

THE JENA CAMPAIGN: 1806 by *F. N. Maude*—The Twin Battles of Jena & Auerstadt Between Napoleon's French and the Prussian Army.

PRIVATE O'NEIL by *Charles O'Neil*—The recollections of an Irish Rogue of H. M. 28th Regt.—The Slashers—during the Peninsula & Waterloo campaigns of the Napoleonic war.

ROYAL HIGHLANDER by *James Anton*—A soldier of H.M 42nd (Royal) Highlanders during the Peninsular, South of France & Waterloo Campaigns of the Napoleonic Wars.

CAPTAIN BLAZE by *Elzéar Blaze*—Life in Napoleons Army.

LEJEUNE VOLUME 1 by *Louis-François Lejeune*—The Napoleonic Wars through the Experiences of an Officer on Berthier's Staff.

LEJEUNE VOLUME 2 by *Louis-François Lejeune*—The Napoleonic Wars through the Experiences of an Officer on Berthier's Staff.

CAPTAIN COIGNET by *Jean-Roch Coignet*—A Soldier of Napoleon's Imperial Guard from the Italian Campaign to Russia and Waterloo.

FUSILIER COOPER by *John S. Cooper*—Experiences in the 7th (Royal) Fusiliers During the Peninsular Campaign of the Napoleonic Wars and the American Campaign to New Orleans.

FIGHTING NAPOLEON'S EMPIRE by *Joseph Anderson*—The Campaigns of a British Infantryman in Italy, Egypt, the Peninsular & the West Indies During the Napoleonic Wars.

CHASSEUR BARRES by *Jean-Baptiste Barres*—The experiences of a French Infantryman of the Imperial Guard at Austerlitz, Jena, Eylau, Friedland, in the Peninsular, Lutzen, Bautzen, Zinnwald and Hanau during the Napoleonic Wars.

AVAILABLE ONLINE AT www.leonaur.com
AND FROM ALL GOOD BOOK STORES

ALSO FROM LEONAUR
AVAILABLE IN SOFTCOVER OR HARDCOVER WITH DUST JACKET

CAPTAIN COIGNET *by Jean-Roch Coignet*—A Soldier of Napoleon's Imperial Guard from the Italian Campaign to Russia and Waterloo.

HUSSAR ROCCA *by Albert Jean Michel de Rocca*—A French cavalry officer's experiences of the Napoleonic Wars and his views on the Peninsular Campaigns against the Spanish, British And Guerilla Armies.

MARINES TO 95TH (RIFLES) *by Thomas Fernyhough*—The military experiences of Robert Fernyhough during the Napoleonic Wars.

LIGHT BOB *by Robert Blakeney*—The experiences of a young officer in H.M 28th & 36th regiments of the British Infantry during the Peninsular Campaign of the Napoleonic Wars 1804 - 1814.

WITH WELLINGTON'S LIGHT CAVALRY *by William Tomkinson*—The Experiences of an officer of the 16th Light Dragoons in the Peninsular and Waterloo campaigns of the Napoleonic Wars.

SERGEANT BOURGOGNE *by Adrien Bourgogne*—With Napoleon's Imperial Guard in the Russian Campaign and on the Retreat from Moscow 1812 - 13.

SURTEES OF THE 95TH (RIFLES) *by William Surtees*—A Soldier of the 95th (Rifles) in the Peninsular campaign of the Napoleonic Wars.

SWORDS OF HONOUR *by Henry Newbolt & Stanley L. Wood*—The Careers of Six Outstanding Officers from the Napoleonic Wars, the Wars for India and the American Civil War.

ENSIGN BELL IN THE PENINSULAR WAR *by George Bell*—The Experiences of a young British Soldier of the 34th Regiment 'The Cumberland Gentlemen' in the Napoleonic wars.

HUSSAR IN WINTER *by Alexander Gordon*—A British Cavalry Officer during the retreat to Corunna in the Peninsular campaign of the Napoleonic Wars.

THE COMPLEAT RIFLEMAN HARRIS *by Benjamin Harris as told to and transcribed by Captain Henry Curling, 52nd Regt. of Foot*—The adventures of a soldier of the 95th (Rifles) during the Peninsular Campaign of the Napoleonic Wars.

THE ADVENTURES OF A LIGHT DRAGOON *by George Farmer & G.R. Gleig*—A cavalryman during the Peninsular & Waterloo Campaigns, in captivity & at the siege of Bhurtpore, India.

AVAILABLE ONLINE AT **www.leonaur.com**
AND FROM ALL GOOD BOOK STORES

ALSO FROM LEONAUR

AVAILABLE IN SOFTCOVER OR HARDCOVER WITH DUST JACKET

THE LIFE OF THE REAL BRIGADIER GERARD VOLUME 1—THE YOUNG HUSSAR 1782-1807 *by Jean-Baptiste De Marbot*—A French Cavalryman Of the Napoleonic Wars at Marengo, Austerlitz, Jena, Eylau & Friedland.

THE LIFE OF THE REAL BRIGADIER GERARD VOLUME 2—IMPERIAL AIDE-DE-CAMP 1807-1811 *by Jean-Baptiste De Marbot*—A French Cavalryman of the Napoleonic Wars at Saragossa, Landshut, Ecknuhl, Ratisbon, Aspern-Essling, Wagram, Busaco & Torres Vedras.

THE LIFE OF THE REAL BRIGADIER GERARD VOLUME 3—COLONEL OF CHASSEURS 1811-1815 *by Jean-Baptiste De Marbot*—A French Cavalryman in the retreat from Moscow, Lutzen, Bautzen, Katzbach, Leipzig, Hanau & Waterloo.

THE INDIAN WAR OF 1864 *by Eugene Ware*—The Experiences of a Young Officer of the 7th Iowa Cavalry on the Western Frontier During the Civil War.

THE MARCH OF DESTINY *by Charles E. Young & V. Devinny*—Dangers of the Trail in 1865 by Charles E. Young & The Story of a Pioneer by V. Devinny, two Accounts of Early Emigrants to Colorado.

CROSSING THE PLAINS *by William Audley Maxwell*—A First Hand Narrative of the Early Pioneer Trail to California in 1857.

CHIEF OF SCOUTS *by William F. Drannan*—A Pilot to Emigrant and Government Trains, Across the Plains of the Western Frontier.

THIRTY-ONE YEARS ON THE PLAINS AND IN THE MOUNTAINS *by William F. Drannan*—William Drannan was born to be a pioneer, hunter, trapper and wagon train guide during the momentous days of the Great American West.

THE INDIAN WARS VOLUNTEER *by William Thompson*—Recollections of the Conflict Against the Snakes, Shoshone, Bannocks, Modocs and Other Native Tribes of the American North West.

THE 4TH TENNESSEE CAVALRY *by George B. Guild*—The Services of Smith's Regiment of Confederate Cavalry by One of its Officers.

COLONEL WORTHINGTON'S SHILOH *by T. Worthington*—The Tennessee Campaign, 1862, by an Officer of the Ohio Volunteers.

FOUR YEARS IN THE SADDLE *by W. L. Curry*—The History of the First Regiment Ohio Volunteer Cavalry in the American Civil War.

AVAILABLE ONLINE AT **www.leonaur.com**
AND FROM ALL GOOD BOOK STORES

ALSO FROM LEONAUR
AVAILABLE IN SOFTCOVER OR HARDCOVER WITH DUST JACKET

LIFE IN THE ARMY OF NORTHERN VIRGINIA by *Carlton McCarthy*—The Observations of a Confederate Artilleryman of Cutshaw's Battalion During the American Civil War 1861-1865.

HISTORY OF THE CAVALRY OF THE ARMY OF THE POTOMAC by *Charles D. Rhodes*—Including Pope's Army of Virginia and the Cavalry Operations in West Virginia During the American Civil War.

CAMP-FIRE AND COTTON-FIELD by *Thomas W. Knox*—A New York Herald Correspondent's View of the American Civil War.

SERGEANT STILLWELL by *Leander Stillwell*—The Experiences of a Union Army Soldier of the 61st Illinois Infantry During the American Civil War.

STONEWALL'S CANNONEER by *Edward A. Moore*—Experiences with the Rockbridge Artillery, Confederate Army of Northern Virginia, During the American Civil War.

THE SIXTH CORPS by *George Stevens*—The Army of the Potomac, Union Army, During the American Civil War.

THE RAILROAD RAIDERS by *William Pittenger*—An Ohio Volunteers Recollections of the Andrews Raid to Disrupt the Confederate Railroad in Georgia During the American Civil War.

CITIZEN SOLDIER by *John Beatty*—An Account of the American Civil War by a Union Infantry Officer of Ohio Volunteers Who Became a Brigadier General.

COX: PERSONAL RECOLLECTIONS OF THE CIVIL WAR--VOLUME 1 by *Jacob Dolson Cox*—West Virginia, Kanawha Valley, Gauley Bridge, Cotton Mountain, South Mountain, Antietam, the Morgan Raid & the East Tennessee Campaign.

COX: PERSONAL RECOLLECTIONS OF THE CIVIL WAR--VOLUME 2 by *Jacob Dolson Cox*—Siege of Knoxville, East Tennessee, Atlanta Campaign, the Nashville Campaign & the North Carolina Campaign.

KERSHAW'S BRIGADE VOLUME 1 by *D. Augustus Dickert*—Manassas, Seven Pines, Sharpsburg (Antietam), Fredricksburg, Chancellorsville, Gettysburg, Chickamauga, Chattanooga, Fort Sanders & Bean Station.

KERSHAW'S BRIGADE VOLUME 2 by *D. Augustus Dickert*—At the wilderness, Cold Harbour, Petersburg, The Shenandoah Valley and Cedar Creek..

AVAILABLE ONLINE AT **www.leonaur.com**
AND FROM ALL GOOD BOOK STORES

ALSO FROM LEONAUR
AVAILABLE IN SOFTCOVER OR HARDCOVER WITH DUST JACKET

THE RELUCTANT REBEL *by William G. Stevenson*—A young Kentuckian's experiences in the Confederate Infantry & Cavalry during the American Civil War..

BOOTS AND SADDLES *by Elizabeth B. Custer*—The experiences of General Custer's Wife on the Western Plains.

FANNIE BEERS' CIVIL WAR *by Fannie A. Beers*—A Confederate Lady's Experiences of Nursing During the Campaigns & Battles of the American Civil War.

LADY SALE'S AFGHANISTAN *by Florentia Sale*—An Indomitable Victorian Lady's Account of the Retreat from Kabul During the First Afghan War.

THE TWO WARS OF MRS DUBERLY *by Frances Isabella Duberly*—An Intrepid Victorian Lady's Experience of the Crimea and Indian Mutiny.

THE REBELLIOUS DUCHESS *by Paul F. S. Dermoncourt*—The Adventures of the Duchess of Berri and Her Attempt to Overthrow French Monarchy.

LADIES OF WATERLOO *by Charlotte A. Eaton, Magdalene de Lancey & Juana Smith*—The Experiences of Three Women During the Campaign of 1815: Waterloo Days by Charlotte A. Eaton, A Week at Waterloo by Magdalene de Lancey & Juana's Story by Juana Smith.

TWO YEARS BEFORE THE MAST *by Richard Henry Dana. Jr.*—The account of one young man's experiences serving on board a sailing brig—the Penelope—bound for California, between the years 1834-36.

A SAILOR OF KING GEORGE *by Frederick Hoffman*—From Midshipman to Captain—Recollections of War at Sea in the Napoleonic Age 1793-1815.

LORDS OF THE SEA *by A. T. Mahan*—Great Captains of the Royal Navy During the Age of Sail.

COGGESHALL'S VOYAGES: VOLUME 1 *by George Coggeshall*—The Recollections of an American Schooner Captain.

COGGESHALL'S VOYAGES: VOLUME 2 *by George Coggeshall*—The Recollections of an American Schooner Captain.

TWILIGHT OF EMPIRE *by Sir Thomas Ussher & Sir George Cockburn*—Two accounts of Napoleon's Journeys in Exile to Elba and St. Helena: Narrative of Events by Sir Thomas Ussher & Napoleon's Last Voyage: Extract of a diary by Sir George Cockburn.

AVAILABLE ONLINE AT www.leonaur.com
AND FROM ALL GOOD BOOK STORES

ALSO FROM LEONAUR
AVAILABLE IN SOFTCOVER OR HARDCOVER WITH DUST JACKET

ESCAPE FROM THE FRENCH by *Edward Boys*—A Young Royal Navy Midshipman's Adventures During the Napoleonic War.

THE VOYAGE OF H.M.S. PANDORA by *Edward Edwards R. N. & George Hamilton, edited by Basil Thomson*—In Pursuit of the Mutineers of the Bounty in the South Seas—1790-1791.

MEDUSA by *J. B. Henry Savigny and Alexander Correard and Charlotte-Adélaïde Dard*—Narrative of a Voyage to Senegal in 1816 & The Sufferings of the Picard Family After the Shipwreck of the Medusa.

THE SEA WAR OF 1812 VOLUME 1 by *A. T. Mahan*—A History of the Maritime Conflict.

THE SEA WAR OF 1812 VOLUME 2 by *A. T. Mahan*—A History of the Maritime Conflict.

WETHERELL OF H. M. S. HUSSAR by *John Wetherell*—The Recollections of an Ordinary Seaman of the Royal Navy During the Napoleonic Wars.

THE NAVAL BRIGADE IN NATAL by *C. R. N. Burne*—With the Guns of H. M. S. Terrible & H. M. S. Tartar during the Boer War 1899-1900.

THE VOYAGE OF H. M. S. BOUNTY by *William Bligh*—The True Story of an 18th Century Voyage of Exploration and Mutiny.

SHIPWRECK! by *William Gilly*—The Royal Navy's Disasters at Sea 1793-1849.

KING'S CUTTERS AND SMUGGLERS: 1700-1855 by *E. Keble Chatterton*—A unique period of maritime history-from the beginning of the eighteenth to the middle of the nineteenth century when British seamen risked all to smuggle valuable goods from wool to tea and spirits from and to the Continent.

CONFEDERATE BLOCKADE RUNNER by *John Wilkinson*—The Personal Recollections of an Officer of the Confederate Navy.

NAVAL BATTLES OF THE NAPOLEONIC WARS by *W. H. Fitchett*—Cape St. Vincent, the Nile, Cadiz, Copenhagen, Trafalgar & Others.

PRISONERS OF THE RED DESERT by *R. S. Gwatkin-Williams*—The Adventures of the Crew of the Tara During the First World War.

U-BOAT WAR 1914-1918 by *James B. Connolly/Karl von Schenk*—Two Contrasting Accounts from Both Sides of the Conflict at Sea During the Great War.

AVAILABLE ONLINE AT **www.leonaur.com**
AND FROM ALL GOOD BOOK STORES

ALSO FROM LEONAUR
AVAILABLE IN SOFTCOVER OR HARDCOVER WITH DUST JACKET

IRON TIMES WITH THE GUARDS *by An O. E. (G. P. A. Fildes)*—The Experiences of an Officer of the Coldstream Guards on the Western Front During the First World War.

THE GREAT WAR IN THE MIDDLE EAST: 1 *by W. T. Massey*—The Desert Campaigns & How Jerusalem Was Won---two classic accounts in one volume.

THE GREAT WAR IN THE MIDDLE EAST: 2 *by W. T. Massey*—Allenby's Final Triumph.

SMITH-DORRIEN *by Horace Smith-Dorrien*—Isandlwhana to the Great War.

1914 *by Sir John French*—The Early Campaigns of the Great War by the British Commander.

GRENADIER *by E. R. M. Fryer*—The Recollections of an Officer of the Grenadier Guards throughout the Great War on the Western Front.

BATTLE, CAPTURE & ESCAPE *by George Pearson*—The Experiences of a Canadian Light Infantryman During the Great War.

DIGGERS AT WAR *by R. Hugh Knyvett & G. P. Cuttriss*—"Over There" With the Australians by R. Hugh Knyvett and Over the Top With the Third Australian Division by G. P. Cuttriss. Accounts of Australians During the Great War in the Middle East, at Gallipoli and on the Western Front.

HEAVY FIGHTING BEFORE US *by George Brenton Laurie*—The Letters of an Officer of the Royal Irish Rifles on the Western Front During the Great War.

THE CAMELIERS *by Oliver Hogue*—A Classic Account of the Australians of the Imperial Camel Corps During the First World War in the Middle East.

RED DUST *by Donald Black*—A Classic Account of Australian Light Horsemen in Palestine During the First World War.

THE LEAN, BROWN MEN *by Angus Buchanan*—Experiences in East Africa During the Great War with the 25th Royal Fusiliers—the Legion of Frontiersmen.

THE NIGERIAN REGIMENT IN EAST AFRICA *by W. D. Downes*—On Campaign During the Great War 1916-1918.

THE 'DIE-HARDS' IN SIBERIA *by John Ward*—With the Middlesex Regiment Against the Bolsheviks 1918-19.

ALSO FROM LEONAUR

AVAILABLE IN SOFTCOVER OR HARDCOVER WITH DUST JACKET

FARAWAY CAMPAIGN by *F. James*—Experiences of an Indian Army Cavalry Officer in Persia & Russia During the Great War.

REVOLT IN THE DESERT by *T. E. Lawrence*—An account of the experiences of one remarkable British officer's war from his own perspective.

MACHINE-GUN SQUADRON by *A. M. G.*—The 20th Machine Gunners from British Yeomanry Regiments in the Middle East Campaign of the First World War.

A GUNNER'S CRUSADE by *Antony Bluett*—The Campaign in the Desert, Palestine & Syria as Experienced by the Honourable Artillery Company During the Great War.

DESPATCH RIDER by *W. H. L. Watson*—The Experiences of a British Army Motorcycle Despatch Rider During the Opening Battles of the Great War in Europe.

TIGERS ALONG THE TIGRIS by *E. J. Thompson*—The Leicestershire Regiment in Mesopotamia During the First World War.

HEARTS & DRAGONS by *Charles R. M. F. Crutwell*—The 4th Royal Berkshire Regiment in France and Italy During the Great War, 1914-1918.

INFANTRY BRIGADE: 1914 by *John Ward*—The Diary of a Commander of the 15th Infantry Brigade, 5th Division, British Army, During the Retreat from Mons.

DOING OUR 'BIT' by *Ian Hay*—Two Classic Accounts of the Men of Kitchener's 'New Army' During the Great War including *The First 100,000 & All In It*.

AN EYE IN THE STORM by *Arthur Ruhl*—An American War Correspondent's Experiences of the First World War from the Western Front to Gallipoli-and Beyond.

STAND & FALL by *Joe Cassells*—With the Middlesex Regiment Against the Bolsheviks 1918-19.

RIFLEMAN MACGILL'S WAR by *Patrick MacGill*—A Soldier of the London Irish During the Great War in Europe including *The Amateur Army, The Red Horizon & The Great Push*.

WITH THE GUNS by *C. A. Rose & Hugh Dalton*—Two First Hand Accounts of British Gunners at War in Europe During World War 1- Three Years in France with the Guns and With the British Guns in Italy.

THE BUSH WAR DOCTOR by *Robert V. Dolbey*—The Experiences of a British Army Doctor During the East African Campaign of the First World War.

AVAILABLE ONLINE AT **www.leonaur.com**
AND FROM ALL GOOD BOOK STORES

ALSO FROM LEONAUR
AVAILABLE IN SOFTCOVER OR HARDCOVER WITH DUST JACKET

THE 9TH—THE KING'S (LIVERPOOL REGIMENT) IN THE GREAT WAR 1914 - 1918 *by Enos H. G. Roberts*—Mersey to mud—war and Liverpool men.

THE GAMBARDIER *by Mark Severn*—The experiences of a battery of Heavy artillery on the Western Front during the First World War.

FROM MESSINES TO THIRD YPRES *by Thomas Floyd*—A personal account of the First World War on the Western front by a 2/5th Lancashire Fusilier.

THE IRISH GUARDS IN THE GREAT WAR - VOLUME 1 *by Rudyard Kipling*—Edited and Compiled from Their Diaries and Papers—The First Battalion.

THE IRISH GUARDS IN THE GREAT WAR - VOLUME 1 *by Rudyard Kipling*—Edited and Compiled from Their Diaries and Papers—The Second Battalion.

ARMOURED CARS IN EDEN *by K. Roosevelt*—An American President's son serving in Rolls Royce armoured cars with the British in Mesopotamia & with the American Artillery in France during the First World War.

CHASSEUR OF 1914 *by Marcel Dupont*—Experiences of the twilight of the French Light Cavalry by a young officer during the early battles of the great war in Europe.

TROOP HORSE & TRENCH *by R.A. Lloyd*—The experiences of a British Lifeguardsman of the household cavalry fighting on the western front during the First World War 1914-18.

THE EAST AFRICAN MOUNTED RIFLES *by C.J. Wilson*—Experiences of the campaign in the East African bush during the First World War.

THE LONG PATROL *by George Berrie*—A Novel of Light Horsemen from Gallipoli to the Palestine campaign of the First World War.

THE FIGHTING CAMELIERS *by Frank Reid*—The exploits of the Imperial Camel Corps in the desert and Palestine campaigns of the First World War.

STEEL CHARIOTS IN THE DESERT *by S. C. Rolls*—The first world war experiences of a Rolls Royce armoured car driver with the Duke of Westminster in Libya and in Arabia with T.E. Lawrence.

WITH THE IMPERIAL CAMEL CORPS IN THE GREAT WAR *by Geoffrey Inchbald*—The story of a serving officer with the British 2nd battalion against the Senussi and during the Palestine campaign.

AVAILABLE ONLINE AT **www.leonaur.com**
AND FROM ALL GOOD BOOK STORES

Lightning Source UK Ltd.
Milton Keynes UK
UKOW02f1859180416

272516UK00001B/30/P